CONTENTS

PREFACE

The story of Master C is a story of serendipity. In January of 1987 a few of us were discussing what the computer book of the future might be like. We decided it would NOT be just a CD ROM, that was too elementary and it was not taking advantage of the power of the computer to simulate a real teacher. No, we decided the book of the future would be a "teacher-on-a-disk." The software would be smart enough to teach you and test you, to probe for your weaknesses, it would be very tolerant of mistakes and would present the same question in many ways. At the same time it would let you read its pages (or screens) just like a real book. It would be structured like a book, but unlike the book it would offer many ways to enter into the learning experience. We thought about our best selling book, *C Primer Plus* (300,000 copies sold), and wondered how we could meld its proven contents with the power of an IBM PC-based delivery system.

A few days later a teacher and part-time software developer in Canada sent me a letter with an interesting idea. He had developed a computer-based teaching system that was being used at four different community colleges. He was using *C Primer Plus*, really liked it, and wanted to create a PC based training course for it. His system sounded exactly like what we had in mind.

After over 2 years of total development we believe that Master C is the first of a new generation of software teaching systems that will eventually replace the book as we know it. We plan to continue to perfect Master C, adding a windowing system, color graphics, animation, and multimedia sound and video. At the same time we will be perfecting our techniques for using artificial intelligence to make Master C the most masterful teacher we can.

I would like to thank the following individuals for helping with the development of Master C: Rex Woollard for unfaltering programming implementation of the courseware and his always helpful and optimistic attitude, David Easley for digging out bugs and bringing us the knowledge of how software is tested, Scott Calamar for editing the manual and helping with the management of the development cycle, Joel Fugazzotto for unrelenting technical support and production coordination, Earl Young for testing the software, Harry Henderson for writing, and for reviewing the software, Barbara Gelfand for cover design and the internal design of the book, Merrill Peterson for production management, Michael Whelan for exciting cover art, and Nick for growling at bill collectors.

Mitchell Waite, June 1990

INTRODUCTION TO THIS BOOK

This book is designed to get you up and running with Master C, a product that turns an IBM PC or compatible into a friendly and intelligent C instructor.

The book is divided into two parts. The first part is a basic manual for Master C; it explains what Master C is, the hardware requirements to use it, Master C's features, how to install and use it, details on exploring Master C for optimum learning, and a map of the course material provided by Master C. It presents an overview of the contents of each "chapter" in Master C, the objectives of the chapter, and an estimate of how long the chapter will take to complete. A chapter describes what to do in case you have trouble installing or using Master C. There is also a chapter on Tips and Tricks to improve your use of Master C.

The second part of this book is a detailed reference to ANSI C. It is designed to allow you to look up any keyword in the C language. The reference chapter gives a definition, syntax description, example call, and other details of using the keyword. You can use the alphabetical references when you need to quickly look up a C function you can't remember, or when you are away from the computer and wish to study or review C's vocabulary.

We recommend that you read Chapter 2 completely before installing the Master C software so you can become well acquainted with Master C's functions. Then install Master C on your PC and begin learning C. There are numerous tips that will make using Master C easier; these are covered in the chapter called *Exploring Master C.* If you have any problems with Master C you are welcome to call the offices of The Waite Group. Please have your registration number available and a detailed description of the problem.

I

Master C Operation

Chapter 1 ➤ WHAT IS MASTER C

Master C is one of the first commercial examples of the computer turned into a teacher; it is designed to teach you all the essential elements of the finalized ANSI C standard. Master C explains everything from the origins of C, running C programs, prototypes and data types, to complex data structures, pointers, and file handling. When you complete the lessons in Master C you will have covered all the topics fundamental to being a proficient C programmer. Much of Master C's contents come from our best-selling book, *The Waite Group's New C Primer Plus* (Howard W. Sams and Company, ISBN 0-672-22687-1, Carmel, IN, $26.95). Master C also parallels our C textbook *The Waite Group's C: Step by Step* (Sams, ISBN 0-672-22651-0, $27.95).

Nearly all the examples in Master C are "generic" C; that is, they're meant to run on any standard C implementation, including all those that compile for the IBM PC, as well as those that compile for minicomputers and mainframe computers. We've tested the program on a VAX 11/750 computer running under BSD 4.3 UNIX and on an IBM AT clone, IBM PC 386 clone, and a standard IBM PC XT using Microsoft 5.1 C, Microsoft QuickC, and Borland Turbo C, and under MS-DOS versions 3.2, 3.3, and 4.0. Occasionally, Master C discusses implementation-dependent matters, such as the differences between the way files are stored. However, we've confined our remarks to UNIX, MS-DOS/PC-DOS, which are currently the two most common environments.

Features of Master C

Master C has evolved over a period of several years. The underlying software engine was developed during five years of research at three educational institutions. The content of Master C was derived from a book with four years of educational and private use and resulting feedback. By blending this powerful software engine with the excellent writing of a proven book, The Waite Group has created an effective learning tool. Here are some of Master C's features.

Student Control

Master C is based on tutorial chapters that are presented as a sequence of text screens. After reading the screens, Master C asks questions and finds out if you understand the topic. The questions may be true/false,

➤ One of the beauties of Master C is that it can ask the same question in different ways.

multiple choice, or fill-in-the-blank. Often the questions are repeated in different ways. One time a question might require a complete word to be typed in, another time it may be presented in true/false format. One of the beauties of Master C is that it can change its questions to make sure you are really thinking.

Master C moves you through the tutorials along a predefined path. If you have trouble answering questions, Master C goes into the *Recall* mode, and "sends" you to the point in the tutorial where your knowledge is weak. After you successfully complete the recalled lesson you return to where you stumbled and then proceed with additional material.

Strategies to Using Master C

There are several strategies for using Master C .

Using Master C Like A Book

The most obvious way is to use Master C like a regular book, starting at the beginning and moving through its material in a linear manner, from Chapter 1 to Chapter 15. Switching to the book, *The Waite Group's New C Primer Plus*, when you are away from the computer, has been anticipated; the book and software completely parallel each other.

Jumping Directly to Tutorials

A real strength of Master C is that it is possible to jump directly to those C topics that are of interest to you. This will allow you to skip the preliminary sections of instruction and move right into the areas you want to understand. Master C will analyze your work in the review lessons, and if you are still wrong, it will send you to the proper lesson, so you can't leave the course confused. Master C tailors the instruction to the particular strengths and weaknesses of each user, something no book can do.

Once inside a Master C lesson, you have control over moving forward and backward through the material. Forward refers to moving from one page (screen) to the next, while backward is like turning pages (screens) backward. At any time you can branch off to use other related Master C features, and you will always be returned to your original position when done.

Studying a Single Concept via the Master C Glossary

Master C's built-in glossary provides a third way to access C knowledge. After looking up a related C word in Master C's glossary, you can request a lesson on the defined word. This can provide a special training path that is finely tuned to what you want to learn.

Using Master C's Review Sections

If you already think you know C and just want to check your knowledge for weaknesses, you can use the Review sections of each Chapter. These Reviews present a condensed summary of the content of the chapter, along with quizzes to test your understanding. Since taking the entire course can consume several days of work, the Reviews provide a quick way to avoid the need for studying certain chapters.

Sophisticated Answer Judging

Master C's skills are most apparent in the way it assesses your responses. Master C is designed to accept a wide range of possible user responses. You can misspell the answer, abbreviate it, and even give the answer in a poorly structured sentence, and Master C will still recognize if the answer is correct. Some questions are open-ended; there are many ways to phrase a correct response. Master C is able to figure out what you mean if you are close. This is unlike most computer-based training systems, which require you to type the exact answer to move forward.

➤ With Master C you can misspell the answer, abbreviate it, and even give the answer in a poorly structured sentence.

Retains Student Progress Information

As you complete various lessons, Master C retains information about your progress. When you ask for a list of your achievements, Master C will tell you which lessons have been completed and what your "score" is. The score is the percentage of correct answers, with 80% being considered "mastery." Master C will also tell you what lessons you have finished, and which you still need to work on.

Digital Bookmarks

You can quit Master C at almost any point in its tutorials. When you return later, Master C will take you back to the exact point in the lesson in which you were last working.

Meaningful Feedback on Wrong Answers

Master C's feedback on answers varies depending on the nature of the questions. With particularly easy questions, a wrong answer causes the system to respond immediately.

With more demanding questions, Master C brings more of its expertise to bear. For example, if you answer a question incorrectly, the answer is analyzed and checked against anticipated problem areas. The system then responds with relevant hints designed to help you clarify your understanding. You will then be given an opportunity to try the question again.

In some cases, if you are still having difficulty with a particular question, Master C will present the same question in an easier form; displayed along with a number of alternative answers, only one of which will be correct. If you get the multiple choice question correct, Master C will deem you to have answered the question correctly. If you have trouble with the multiple choice question, Master C will switch into the Recall mode.

Recall Mode

Master C 's recall mode is one of its most powerful learning elements. Following the presentation of a question and the subsequent answer analysis and helpful hints, you might still be having difficulty with a particular topic. Here, Master C will automatically return to a tutorial lesson covering that topic. You will then have a chance to review this related material before trying to answer the question again.

On-line Glossary

Because you may encounter unfamiliar terms or keywords, Master C includes an on-line Glossary. At any point in the course, you can look up related C terms for additional information. Master C will even attempt to match close spellings when you are unsure of the exact term. With many of the terms, the glossary will offer to link you to related instructional material. If you choose to work with the related material, afterward you will be able to return to your jumping off-point—the place where you first invoked the glossary.

This feature provides an alternate and powerful learning path. Ordinarily, you are likely to access learning material by choosing lesson items from a menu. Using the glossary, you can jump directly to instructional material by entering the desired term or keyword. There is no need to walk back and forth through menus. This feature is useful in a variety of circumstances. In one case, you may already be familiar with the C language, but need to reference the learning material on some specific topic. Using the glossary, you can jump directly to the appropriate subsection from anywhere in the course. You don't have to use the menus at all.

➤ The glossary mode allows you to hunt down a specific concept and really understand it.

Even if you are using the menus as your primary path to learning material, you can make good use of the glossary path. Imagine that you are working through a lesson dealing with control loops, and you encounter references to the ++ operator. Without leaving the lesson on loops, you can use the glossary to explore other lessons covering the ++ operator. When finished with the ++ operator, you will automatically be brought back to your jumping off point—the lesson on loops. You can pick up from where you left off.

Calculator

An on-line 9-digit, scientific calculator is also included. It supports standard trig functions and constants such as *pi*. It does not do pointer arithmetic nor allow you to do segment math for the Intel family of microprocessors.

Chapter 2 ➤ INSTALLING MASTER C

System Requirements

This package can be installed on virtually any MS-DOS based machine. The minimum system configuration is an IBM PC, XT, AT or compatible, with 384K of RAM, a floppy drive, a hard drive, and a monochrome screen which supports highlighting. Though a monochrome monitor is sufficient, Master C takes best advantage of a color monitor which is much easier to read. When installed on the hard disk, approximately 2.2 megabytes of storage is required for Master C.

Overview of Installation

➤ Master C's files are compressed, so you must run Install. About 2.2 megabytes of hard disk space are required.

Master C is easy to install. The core programs and their associated data files are supplied on four 360K IBM PC floppy disks in a compressed format. Because we have used a compressed format, you must use the INSTALL program on Master C Disk 1 to get Master C up and running—simply copying the files will not work.

The first time you install Master C you will be asked to enter your name and the serial number printed on Disk One. Your copy of Master C will then be updated to include this registration information. Later, if you choose to install Master C on another computer system, the registration information will already be recorded; you will not be asked to enter your name and serial number again. *Master C can legally only be used on one computer system at a time. Be sure and fill out and mail in the enclosed registration card.*

ANSI.SYS and NANSI.SYS

Master C requires a device driver, such as ANSI.SYS, installed in your PC in order to properly use the screen. ANSI.SYS comes with all versions of PC-DOS and MS-DOS. However, many people may not have ANSI.SYS installed on their PC. Don't worry if you don't have ANSI.SYS installed. The Master C installation process automatically loads an ANSI.SYS compatible driver called NANSI.SYS, to your root directory, and creates a copy of your CONFIG.SYS file that contains the additional line DEVICE = NANSI.SYS. (Your old CONFIG.SYS is saved as CONFIG.BAK.) Once you restart the computer, this installation method will make Master C work. By the way, NANSI.SYS is actually faster than ANSI.SYS when writing to the screen, so you may prefer to use it instead of ANSI.SYS.

If you have ANSI.SYS already installed, or prefer to use it instead of Master C's NANSI.SYS, you can restore your old CONFIG.SYS file with the DOS command

COPY CONFIG.BAK CONFIG.SYS. Enter

You can then eliminate the file NANSI.SYS with

DEL NANSI.SYS. Enter

If you want to use ANSI.SYS, make sure that it resides on the hard disk and that the command DEVICE = ANSI.SYS is in your CONFIG.SYS file. If ANSI.SYS is in a directory, such as DRIVERS, make sure the device name statement in CONFIG.SYS is

DEVICE = C:\DRIVERS\ANSI.SYS.

Before Installing Master C

Before starting this installation make sure you have at least 2.2 megabytes of free space on your hard disk to hold the Master C files.

Steps for the First Installation

As a first step, take a moment to record the serial number of Master C Disk One in this guide.

➤ **Master C contains a serial number that identifies it as your copy.**

Write your serial number from Disk One ________________________
You will be asked to enter this number during the first installation.

1. Start your computer.

2. Place Disk 1 in the A: drive (you can also use drive B:).

3. Select drive A: by typing: **A:** Enter

4. Start the INSTALL program by typing: **INSTALL** Enter

5. The first screen, shown in Figure 1, will display the Master C logo screen, overlaid with a dialog box that requests you to enter your first and last names, and the serial number on Master C Disk 1. Following this step, your copy of Master C will be permanently registered in your name. Note you must enter a valid name and serial number or Master C will not be installed.

Figure 1: The opening screen for the install program. You must enter your name and serial number.

6. As the installation program proceeds, explanations will appear and you will be asked to insert each of the subsequent Master C disks. You will also be able to choose the drive letter of the hard disk on which you wish to install Master C.

Note: During the installation process, status messages will be displayed to detail the system's progress. These can be ignored unless you encounter problems.

During installation Master C will install a "device driver." Because device drivers are loaded only when the computer is started, you should restart your computer after the installation process is complete. Additional information about device drivers is available in Chapter 6, *In Case of Trouble.*

Steps for a Subsequent Installation

Should you choose to install Master C again, you will follow the same steps which are outlined above, except step 5. Since you will have already registered your copy of Master C, you will not be asked to enter your name and disk serial number a second time.

Chapter 3 ➤ USING MASTER C

Getting Started

You can start Master C from the root directory or from the \MASTERC directory by typing

MASTERC Enter

The first thing you'll see will be the logo screen as shown in Figure 2. It is displayed while several additional program and data files are loaded into your computer.

After the logo screen is displayed, you will see a welcome message inviting you to explore the online introductory tutorial (accessed by typing **T**). Following the welcome you will see the opening Table of

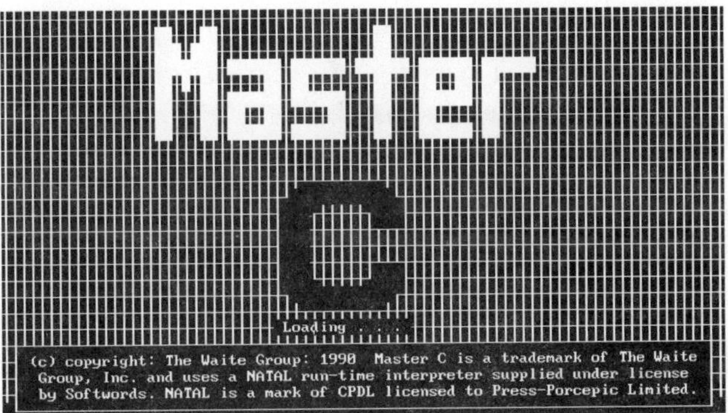

Figure 2: The opening screen for Master C appears immediately after you start the program.

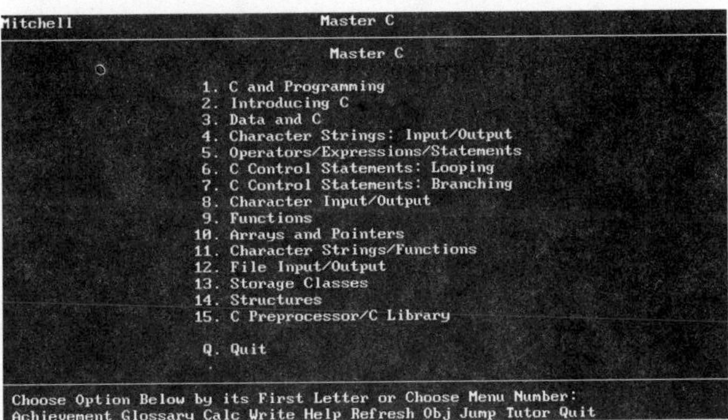

Figure 3: Main Table of Contents screen for Master C. You can access any chapter or command on the option bar.

> ### *If Your Text Doesn't Display Properly*
>
> **Master C assumes you have a color display (CGA or EGA) connected to your computer. However, some IBM PC compatible computers use amber, gray, or green displays. Because Master C uses colors that may be incompatible with certain monochrome displays, you may find that Master C will not initially display bright and non-bright characters properly. If you find your text screen is difficult to read it can be corrected by simply switching Master C to the monochrome display mode. To do this first press the H key to enable the Help window. (H is one of several commands in the Option bar area.) When the Help window is open, press the C key. This will change the Master C Color Map from color to monochrome.** ■

Contents screen for Master C, as shown in Figure 3. This is the main screen or "menu" and is used for accessing the 15 chapters of Master C.

Introductory Tutorial

While at the main table of contents screen, you may wish to try the on-line Tutorial that teaches you how Master C works. The Tutorial is a good way for first–time users to learn how to use Master C. You don't really need to read Chapter 2 any further if you decide to use the on-line Master C Tutorial. To start the Tutorial type **T** Enter.

Adjusting Brightness and Contrast

It is important to set the brightness and contrast correctly since Master C uses highlighted text to emphasize important words and program code. Descriptions and explanations contain highlighted text to identify essential concepts or keywords of the C language. In other cases a large section of program code may be displayed. Here, one or more parts of code will be highlighted—parts which are the current focus of discussion. As you progress through the explanation of the program, the highlighting will shift dynamically to different sections of code to reflect the changing focus of attention.

Before going too far into the tutorial, we suggest you first adjust the brightness and contrast of your text on the screen. As shown in Figure 4, on the first screen of the introductory tutorial you should notice that the word "highlighted" is brighter than the remaining text. If you cannot see a difference, you may have to work with the brightness and

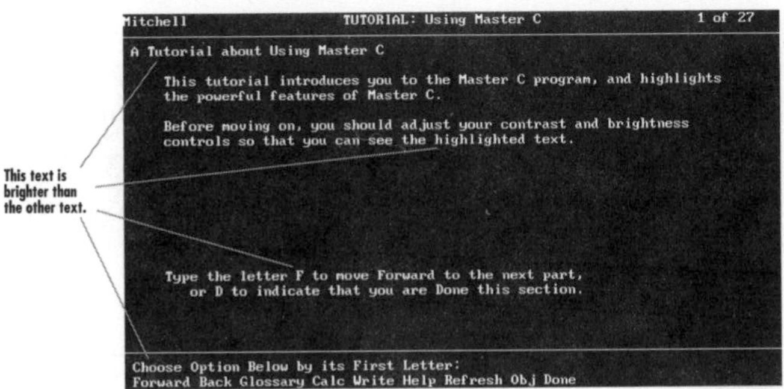

Figure 4: Adjust the brightness of your display so the highlighted areas are brighter.

contrast controls—adjusting one a little, then the other—until a suitable balance is obtained.

The following section describes the components that make up Master C.

Relation of Chapters and Lessons

Before we get too deep into the details of Master C, it will help to understand the organizational relationship between the chapters of *New C Primer Plus* the book (or *C: Step-by-Step*) and the Master C software. In Master C, chapters are made up of text based menus and submenus. These menus roughly follow the various headings of the book.

The Inside on X of Y Screen Numbering

Obviously, the total number of screens varies with each lesson of Master C. That's pretty well expected. But because of the way Master C is designed, the total number of screens may vary for the same given lesson depending on when and how that lesson is entered. Different circumstances lead to different total screen pages.

For example, suppose you are working with lesson 3.4.1 The int Type. You enter this lesson using the menus, and the top right corner of your screen shows *1 of 20.* Each time you enter through the menu, you work through these 20 screens. However, if you answer a question incorrectly after the helpful hints, you will be taken to a small review lesson. This review is also drawn from lesson 3.4.1 The int Type. This time, however, you will review just a subset of the entire lesson; so the top right corner will show *1 of 4.*

Another way the total number of screens for a lesson can change is when you quit after partially completing a lesson. For example, if you quit Master C while on screen 4 of a 20-screen lesson, when you return to the lesson by restarting Master C you will see *1 of 16* in the top right corner. Since you have already successfully completed the first four screens, you will not be presented with them when you return, and only 16 screens will remain. This shows Master C's ability to remember where you left off and give you the most recent statistics. Whenever you reenter a lesson directly from the menu, you will always be presented with the full collection of screens, even if you have worked on the lesson before. ■

We sometimes call the highest level menu the Table of Contents screen. Each item on this menu represents a lesson that corresponds to a chapter in the book. From this menu you may go to the beginning of the lesson for the chapter by typing a number. Each lesson begins with a similar menu, called a sub-menu. These sub-menu screens correspond to the largest typesize heads in *New C Primer Plus.*

Parts of the Screen

Master C presents a consistent screen layout to make "navigation" of the learning system easier. Every screen has three general areas as shown in Figure 5.

- **Main Instructional Area**
- **Top Line**
- **Option Bar**

Each of these areas serves several different functions.

The Main Instructional Area

The large center part of the screen is used to present all instructional material. This material includes explanations, notes, and examples, as well as questions and feedback.

The Top Line

As Figure 5 shows, the area above the top horizontal line, called the Top Line, indicates three things. The left corner displays your first name, which appears on every screen. This is the name that was typed into the "first name" field dialog box when the software was first installed. The name is useful in a classroom environment where it allows a teacher to identify which students are working specifically on Master C.

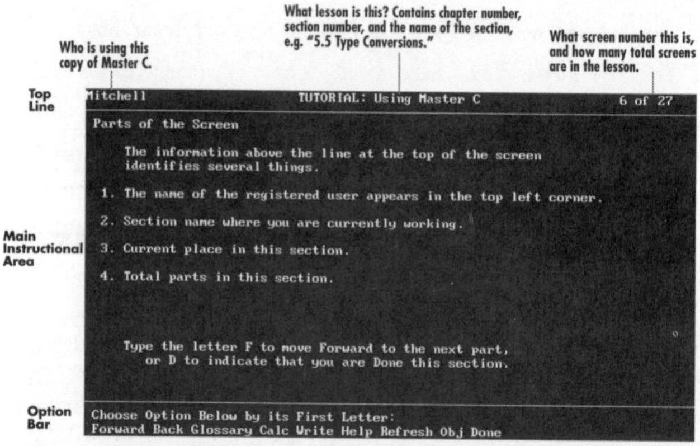

The particular lesson on which you are working is identified in the center portion of the Top Line. In the case of the Tutorial it just shows a title. In the case of a typical screen,

Figure 5: The three parts of the Master C screen.

the title will contain the chapter number (between 1 and 15) for the lesson, the section number within the lesson, and the name of the section. So, for example, *5.5 Type Conversion*, means we are looking at the screen for Chapter 5 (Operators, Expressions, and Statements), section 5 (Type Conversions).

The top right corner of the Top Line always tells you the screen number you are currently viewing and the total number of screens that make up the lesson. Thus *1 of 26* means you are viewing the first screen of a total of 26 screens.

➤ You navigate through Master C's knowledge with the commands in the Option Bar at the bottom of the screen.

The Option Bar

The Option bar appears at the bottom of the screen. It consists of a number of keywords which identify specific functions available as you use Master C. From the Option area you navigate your way through Master C. It allows you to select chapters and topics to study, to move forward and backward through the lesson screens, to explore the glossary, to review your achievements (scores), and so on.

An option is invoked by typing the first letter of its name. For example, to invoke the Help option, you would type **H**, to move Forward you would type **F**, and so on. You don't need to type capitals, lowercase will do.

The actual options appearing in the Option bar change slightly as you use Master C. When a *Note* or *Example* option is available, it appears flashing in the Option bar area. The standard options do not flash.

The Option Bar: Forward and Back

The first two options are invoked by typing **F** for Forward and **B** for Back, the two most common ways of moving through lessons. When you choose to move forward, Master C moves to the next element in the lesson. When more complex concepts are being explored, this involves adding more information to the material already shown in the Main Instructional Area. In other cases, a completely new screen will be generated. You can choose to move back when you wish to review earlier material in the current lesson. The Back option takes you one step at a time to each preceding screen.

Note: If you choose to move back while at the first screen, you will be taken back to the point where you entered the lesson. Usually, this will take you back to a menu, since menu access is the most common path into lessons. If you entered review lesson material after answering a

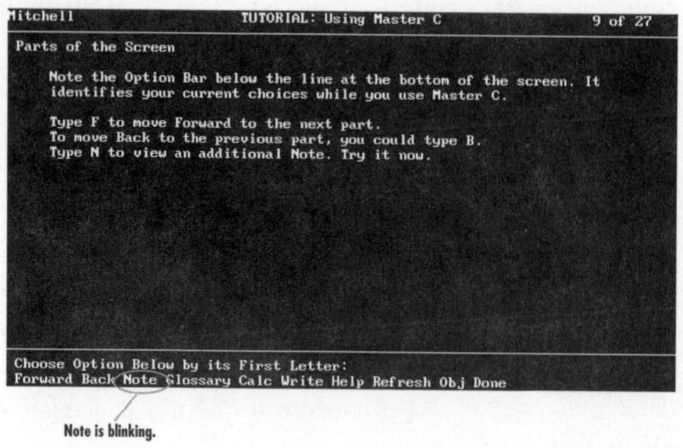

Mitchell
TUTORIAL: Using Master C
9 of 27
Parts of the Screen
Note the Option Bar below the line at the bottom of the screen. It
identifies your current choices while you use Master C.
Type F to move Forward to the next part.
To move Back to the previous part, you could type B.
Type N to view an additional Note. Try it now.
Choose Option Below by its First Letter:
Forward Back Note Glossary Calc Write Help Refresh Obj Done
Note is blinking.

Figure 6a: The Note window item flashing.

question incorrectly, or entered through the glossary, then you would be taken back to that starting point.

The Option Bar: Note and Example

When the options *Note* or *Example* appear flashing in the Option bar area it means you can access an additional window containing related information about the current concept. (See Figures 6a and 6b.)

A *Note* window may contain additional information that further clarifies a point, it might contain the output of a program, or it might be an alternate approach to coding some operation. A *Note* window may address the issue of machine dependency (the differences between UNIX and MS-DOS implementations), it may detail some underlying organization and structure; or it may just be an interesting aside. When *Note* is flashing, its window is displayed by typing **N** for *Note.* Once you have read the *Note* you can erase its window with the **R** (Refresh) key, or move to the next screen (with the **F** (Forward) key) and also remove the window.

An *Example* window usually contains a specific C example, which extends the idea displayed in the main instructional area. This additional information can be viewed by typing **E** when *Example* is flashing as an option in the Option bar.

In both *Notes* and *Examples* windows only a portion of the original main screen information will still be visible behind the windows. To view all of the original main screen information again, you can choose the *Refresh* option by typing **R**.

```
Mitchell                TUTORIAL: Using Master C                  9 of 27
Parts of the Screen
                 NOTE
  Note the Opti  This is an example of a "Note." As you work through this
  identifies yo  course, these notes will contain special information that
                 will help your understanding of C.
  Type F to mov
  To move Back   The Note prompt on the option bar will blink, whenever
  Type N to vie  there is related information available. We recommend that
                 you read the "Note" material.

                 You can type R to erase this note and Refresh the screen,
                 or F to move Forward to the next part. If you type R, the
                 Note prompt will blink again.

Choose Option Below by its First Letter:
Forward Back Glossary Calc Write Help Refresh Obj Done
```

The Note Window

Figure 6b: The Note window enabled.

The Option Bar: Glossary

The Master C Glossary provides online access to a collection of terms and concepts related to the C language. When invoked, you are asked to enter your term and Master C searches for it—trying to match close spellings when an exact match is not found. In Figure 7, we look up the term "%d."

After displaying the related information in the glossary, you are given the opportunity to enter another glossary term. Or you can leave the Glossary mode by pressing the Enter key without entering any term. The glossary information remains on the screen, but you have access to all the items on the Option bar again. You can choose to move Forward or Back, or access any other available option. More uses of the Glossary option are discussed in Chapter 4, *Exploring Master C*.

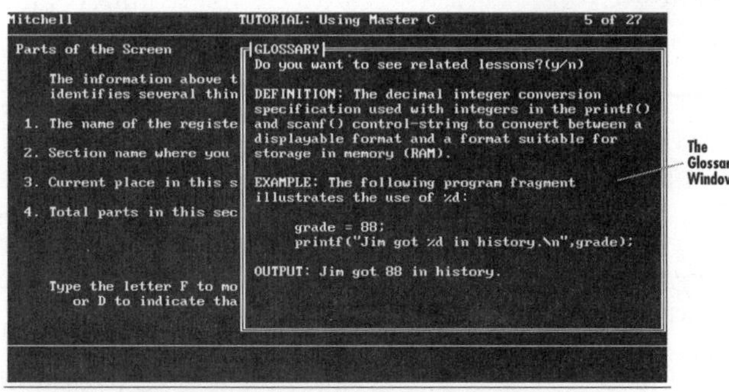

Figure 7: The glossary window enabled.

The Option Bar: Calc

The on-line calculator is called *Calc*. It provides access to trigonometric functions, the constant *pi*, and standard arithmetic operators. In addition, *Calc* supports parentheses and adheres to the rules regarding order of operations. Arithmetic expressions can span more than one line. To enable the *Calc* option type **C**; to exit *Calc* press the Enter key without entering an expression.

The Option Bar: Write

The *Write* option presently displays the address and phone number of The Waite Group, the publishers of Master C. A future version of Master C may use the Write option to allow sending electronic mail to an instructor.

The Option Bar: Help

When working inside a lesson, if you activate *Help* by typing **H**, you are presented with a window giving a small menu of help items and your name and serial number. One help menu item gives a brief description of the function of each of the active options in the Option bar area. Another allows you to change the display from color to monochrome.

The Option Bar: Objective

Activating the *Objective* option by typing **O** brings up a window containing the objective for the current lesson or the menu. The objective is useful in determining the goals of the chapter, and for determining how long the chapter would normally take to complete. As you move from lesson to lesson, you can invoke the objective window to list the essential elements of the active lesson. The information in this window identifies the main topics to be covered, an estimate of the time required to complete the material, and the "mastery" level.

➤ To abort Master C at any time you can type CTRL-C and press Enter twice.

Mastery consists of passing 80% of the questions asked in a chapter. We chose this value because we felt it was the best compromise between just passing knowledge of C (70% Mastery) and a complete understanding of the C language (90%to 100% Mastery).

A few lessons contain no questions because the lessons are introductory in nature. When a lesson has questions, the mastery level will be displayed in the objective window; when there are no questions in a lesson, no mastery level is set or displayed.

The Option Bar: Done and Quit

You may exit from the current lesson—either instructional material or a submenu—by typing **D** to invoke the *Done* option. This will return you to the section of Master C where you were previously located. The *Done* Option will *not* save any achievement information, and you will be asked for a confirmation. You use *Done* when you are reviewing material and don't need to complete all the screens. This may be during a *Recall* mode or when using the Glossary.

When you type **Q** to *Quit* and confirm your choice, you will end your current tutorial session and your achievement information will be saved. When you come back to the tutorials for another session, Master C will return you to the point where you previously exited, using its *bookmark* feature.

You can't quit Master C from certain screens because Quit, **Q**, is not available on the Option bar. For example, if you are in the middle of a question, **Q** won't be available. In such cases you can still abort Master C by typing **CTRL-C** Enter Enter, which will take you back to the DOS command mode, or to the shell interface that was running when you started Master C. You will not get credit for the section you were in when you abort with CTRL-C.

Now that you understand the way Master C navigates, let's find out how the program works, and how to best use it to learn C.

Chapter 4 ➤ EXPLORING MASTER C

Master C uses an age-old method of teaching; it presents facts then it presents questions to see if you really understand the facts. Questions that Master C presents may be fill-in-the-blank, where you must complete a sentence or type in a specific word or phase; multiple choice, where there are three or four possible answers; or true/false. Most teaching software stops here. What is special about Master C is that it alters the way it asks the same question! Note however, that when Master C asks you to enter lines of C code you must be careful about the case; C *is* case sensitive.

Alteration of Question Presentation

If you repeat a question you may be presented with a completely different form of the same question the second time. For example, a question which was presented in a multiple choice form might be presented again in a true/false form.

For example, the first time you take a lesson you might get the question "What is the name of the computer part which can store large amounts of information even when the computer is turned off?". This requires typing in "disk" (however, Master C also accepts "floppy," and several other related answers). The next time you get to this question it might be rephrased as "In a computer, RAM can store large amounts of your information, even when the computer is turned off. True or false?" This question requires a true or false response, yet it is essentially close to the original question. This makes the test more realistic and less repetitive.

➤ You can use abbreviated or shortened answers; Master C is not picky about how you type as long as you are close.

Use Abbreviated and Shortened Answers

Master C asks many questions that are open-ended; there could be many ways to phrase the correct response. This is particularly true with questions presented in a fill-in-the-blank format. Master C allows you to approximate the real answer much as a real teacher would; if your response consists of shortened words or partial phrases that still contain the basic meaning of the answer, it will be judged to be correct. This allows Master C to consider the widest possible range of correct answers and not penalize a user because the answer wasn't typed exactly as the computer expected it.

In the previous example the complete answer is considered to be "floppy or hard disk," but the user can answer "disk," hard drive, "floppy," etc. So when questions deal with definitions and concepts, feel free to use shortened answers. However, when questions deal with the details of C programming code, be sure to include all the elements.

For true/false questions you can also simply type **T** for true and **F** for false; there is no need to spell out the entire word.

Questions that Get Progressively Easier

In some cases, a question may be structured to become progressively easier if you enter an incorrect answer. As a first step, Master C will usually offer some helpful hint—a hint which relates to your particular incorrect answer. As another step of simplification, the question may be presented again, accompanied by a series of possible answers (essentially a multiple choice question).

Suppose you are working through review lesson *2.9 Writing Your First Program* and Master C asks the question:

> *The statement used to include the file stdio.h (which contains basic information about input and output) is:*

If you answer this question by typing:

> *include stdio.h*

which is wrong, Master C will NOT call this wrong, but rather will present a "hint" and give you another chance:

> *You forgot the # symbol*
> *Your answer: include stdio.h*
> *Please try again*

The *Feedback* window will also display what you typed so you can review it and compare it with what Master C says. Next suppose you tried again and typed this answer:

> *#include stdio.h*

This is still wrong, because in C there need to be angle brackets around the file name *stdio.h.* This time Master C recognizes that you are having problems, and like a wise teacher it will still not say you are wrong. Instead Master C will present a multiple-choice question that includes the actual answer:

#include <stdio.h>
#include <stdio.h>;
#include <sutdio>
include <stdio.h>

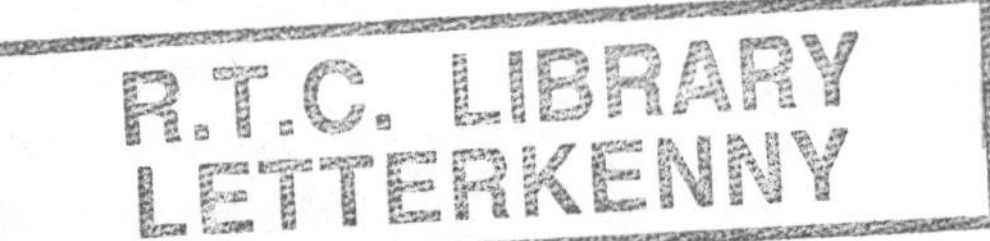

Multiple choice questions are easier than equivalent fill-in-the-blank questions. With a fill-in-the-blank question, you must recall the answer without any cueing. With a similar multiple choice question, you can survey the four choices and select the best answer. In the first case, skills of recall were required; in the second, skills of recognition.

Recognizing Incomplete Answers

Master C employs an interesting technique to accept incomplete answers and prompt you for the remaining parts. For example, suppose Master C asks

> *All C programs begin execution with a function that is always called main. The full answer is:*

and you type

> *main*

Master C will present this text in its Feedback window:

> *Your are correct so far. Continue.*

It is telling you that you have typed in an almost complete answer, but more is still needed. If you follow with (), Master C will say you are correct and move to the next question. If you type the wrong next characters, Master C will judge the answer as incorrect.

➤ The Accumulated Answers window allows you to see the program grow as you move through further questions.

Blackboards: Accumulating Answers Window

The *Accumulating Answers* window provides a way to let you respond to questions that builds a complete C program or program fragment (see Figure 8.) The answers to the questions are C code statements. After each question is answered the resulting code appears in a specialized window called the *Accumulated Answers* window. This window allows you to see the program grow as you move through subsequent questions.

With the *Accumulated Answers* window on the screen, the area allocated for a user's answer is only about half a screen width. However, long typed answers can be continued on the next line.

Mastery Learning

Each time a question is presented in Master C your attempt at an answer is recorded by the software. If you get it right you are given credit for that question. However, if you give the wrong answer, or if you choose to repeat a question (using the Review option), you will be judged as getting the question wrong. Master C's approach is that you must go completely through a lesson and answer at least 80% of the questions correctly (i.e., less than 20% wrong or reviewed). Therefore, if at the end of a Master C lesson you answer less than 80% of the questions correctly, you will need to repeat those questions answered incorrectly to be judged as passing.

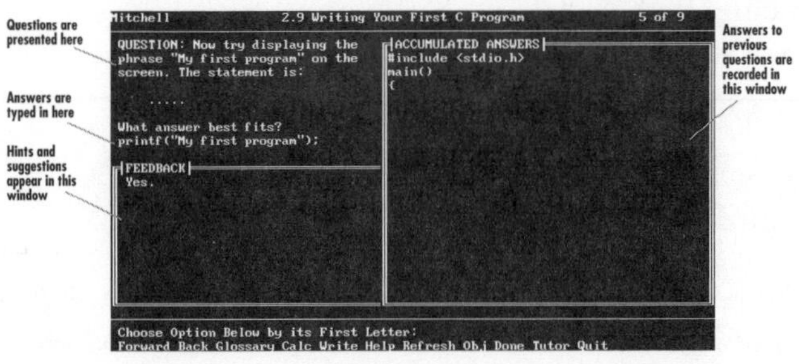

Figure 8: The Accumulated Answer type of question.

Using the Achievement Option

Master C saves a record of your progress in the MASTER C/REGISTER directory files. When you select **A** , the *Achievement* option, Master C searches the two files containing information about your progress. It then displays a short highlighted word or graphic symbol in front of each section, as follows.

80%-100% A number between 80 and 100% indicates that you have successfully completed the lesson. Any score of less than 80% displays the word REPEAT in front of the section.

BEGUN BEGUN indicates that you used the *Done* or *Quit* option to exit from a lesson before its end. BEGUN lets you know that the lesson was started but is not complete.

DONE DONE is displayed in front of those sections which were completed but did not have any questions, and hence had no scores.

REPEAT REPEAT is displayed in front of those sections which were completed with a score of less than 80%.

REVIEWED REVIEWED is displayed in front of those main menu items (i.e. chapters) which were examined via the *Review* menu heading. The individual chapter menu will have a score posted for the *Review* section.

■ A square graphic character is displayed in front of sections that have not been started.

Posting of Achievement

When you successfully complete an entire lesson set (that is, all the lesson items in a chapter) a record of that success will be posted to the originating menu, *but only if you choose the Achievement option on the lower level or the just completed menu.* For example, suppose you complete all lessons in the lesson, 2: *Introducing C.* In order for this information to be posted to the top-level of Master C you must choose the Achievement option before you leave the menu for lesson set 2. This approach is used to speed the processing of Master C. Without it, your movement from menu to menu would be uncomfortably slow.

Resetting Achievement

If you wish to remove all your achievement information (scores) so that you can start Master C over, you must erase the two files in the C:\MASTERC\REGISTER directory. One of these files is named LIST, the other is named whatever you typed into the first name field of the dialog box at installation.

Using the Jump Option

The **J** *Jump* option allows you to jump directly to a lesson by its heading number, without having to walk back and forth through the menus. This feature is particularly useful when you are already familiar with C or when you are using Master C with the book *The Waite Group's C: Step-by-Step.* (*New C Primer Plus* does not have numbered heads.)

Imagine that you wanted to find out more about the *printf* function.

You look *printf* up in the course map found in this book or in the book: *C: Step by Step* and find lesson *4.4.1 Using printf.* After starting Master C, while sitting at any menu, invoke the *Jump* option. When asked to enter the lesson or section number, enter 4.4.1 (note that each of the elements of the number must be separated by a period.)

When you complete the lesson to which you jumped, Master C will return you to your starting point.

Using the Glossary

It is possible to use Master C in a more direct manner than studying its contents lesson by lesson. You can look up a specific concept or keyword in the Glossary, then jump to the location in Master C where that concept or keyword is covered. Master C doesn't just jump from the keyword to a specific concept. Rather it locates only those screens that are relevant to the keyword or concept and presents them.

Using the Review Lessons

The main menu for most chapters in Master C contains a heading called *Review* which can be accessed by typing its item number. If you are somewhat familiar with C programming or you want to test your knowledge before embarking on detailed study in all the lessons, you can use this *Review* item.

As you work through the material, you will be presented with information and asked to answer questions. Whenever you answer a question incorrectly, after prompting by Master C, you will be taken to the parts of earlier lessons where you are weak. This is a quick way to let Master C diagnose your problems and structure an individualized review.

When you complete a *Review* lesson, your success will be posted to the originating menu. The label on the parent menu will show REVIEWED. This is Master C's way of showing the difference between completing all lessons in a menu or only the review lesson.

Embarking on Your Own

We have outlined a number of features of Master C, and suggested a number of strategies for accessing information. The best approach is to use a combination of these techniques, reading sections in a sequence; alternating with reading the book; jumping into specific lessons via the *Glossary*, studying just the *Review* sections.

Chapter 5 ➤ COURSE MAP

The following table shows the average time required by each chapter and the total time for the entire course. In establishing these time estimates, we have assumed that you have worked with some other programming language (though this is not a pre-requisite to learning with Master C). We have also assumed that you will be spending additional time working in a real programming environment so that you can begin to apply your newly acquired skills.

Overview

This is the main menu in Master C. It is also referred to in the manual as the *Table of Contents* menu. This menu provides access to all the chapter menus in the Master C course.

Table 1. Master C Course Time Requirements

Chapter	Master C	Hours
1	*C and Programming*	1.5
2	*Introducing C*	1.5
3	*Data and C*	2.0
4	*Character Strings: Input/Output*	1.75
5	*Operators/Expressions/Statements*	1.5
6	*C Control Statements: Looping*	2.5
7	*C Control Statements: Branching*	3.0
8	*Character Input/Output*	2.0
9	*Functions*	2.5
10	*Arrays and Pointers*	3.5
11	*Character Strings/Functions*	3.5
12	*File Input/Output*	2.0
13	*Storage Classes*	2.0
14	*Structures*	1.25
15	*C Preprocessor/C Library*	0.5
	Total	31.0

1: C AND PROGRAMMING

Objectives

- Learning about C's history and features
- Understanding the steps to programming
- Gaining an overview of structured programming
- Learning what compilers and linkers do
- Knowing what K&R C and ANSI C are

Time Requirements: 1.5 hours

Overview of Contents

Welcome to the world of C. This chapter introduces you to the basics of this powerful and increasingly popular language. We begin by examining briefly C's history and features. Then we discuss the process of programming from a design standpoint and from a practical standpoint. There is more to using a computer language than learning the language rules and the mechanics of creating a program, just as there is more to writing a novel than learning grammar and the use of a keyboard. We introduce you to a productive programming style called structured programming. Finally, we look at the question of language standards.

2: INTRODUCING C

2.1 *A Simple Sample of C*
2.2 *The Explanation*
2.3 *The Structure of a Simple Program*
2.4 *Tips to Make Your Programs Readable*
2.5 *Taking Another Step*
2.6 *Multiple Functions*
2.7 *Debugging*
2.8 *Keywords*
2.9 *Review: Writing Your First Program*

Objectives

- Learning the significance of *main*
- Understanding the structure of a simple program: header, body, braces, and statements
- Declaring an integer variable
- Assigning a value to a variable
- Printing a phrase
- Printing the value of an integer variable
- Using the newline character: *\n*
- Including comments in a program
- Writing simple programs
- Using more than one function in a program
- Debugging simple programs
- Understanding and tracing program states
- Knowing what keywords are

Time Requirements: 1.5 hours

Overview of Contents

What does a C program look like? If you scan through this book, you'll see many examples. Quite likely, you'll find C peculiar looking, sprinkled with symbols like **ptr++*. As you read through this book, you will find that the appearance of these and of other characteristic C symbols grows less cryptic, more familiar, perhaps even welcome! In this chapter we will begin by presenting a rather simple example program and explaining what it does. At the same time we will highlight some of the basic features of C. If you desire detailed elaborations of these features, don't worry. They will come in the following chapters.

3: DATA AND C

Objectives

- Learning the basic C data types: *int, short, long, unsigned, char, float, double, long double*
- Declaring a variable of any type
- Writing integer constants
- Writing character constants
- Using C escape sequences
- Writing floating-point constants
- Using some of the *printf* format specifiers
- Making simple use of *scanf*
- Knowing when to use different data types

Time Requirements: 2 hours

Overview of Contents

Programs work with data. We feed numbers, letters, and words to the computer, and we expect it to do something with the data. In the next two chapters we will concentrate on data concepts and properties. Following that, we begin to examine what we can do with data. But since it is not much fun just talking about data, we will do a little data manipulation in this chapter, too.

The main topics in this chapter are the two great families of data types: integer and floating point. C offers several varieties of these types. We will learn what the types are, how to declare them, how to use them, and when to use them. Also, we will discuss the differences between constants and variables.

4: CHARACTER STRINGS: INPUT/OUTPUT

Objectives

- Understanding the character string
- Writing character strings
- How strings are stored
- Using an array to hold a string
- Using the *strlen* function
- Using *scanf* to read in a string
- Learning the preprocessor *#define* directive
- Using *printf* and *scanf* conversion specifications
- Fine-tuning output formats
- Creating variable-width formats
- Skipping over input

Time Requirements: 1.75 hours

Overview of Contents

In this chapter we'll concentrate on input and output. Programs are more interesting when they can deal with text, so we will begin our study of character strings and how to handle them interactively. We also will take a more detailed look at those two important C I/O functions, *printf* and *scanf.* These will give you the tools to communicate with a C program and to format output to meet your needs and tastes. Also, we'll take a look at an important C facility, the C preprocessor, and learn how to define and use symbolic constants.

5: OPERATORS, EXPRESSIONS, AND STATEMENTS

Objectives

- Understanding what operators and operands are
- Learning several basic operators
- Understanding C expressions
- Evaluating C expressions: operator precedence
- Learning what a C statement is
- Using a *while* loop
- Forming a compound statement, or block
- Learning about automatic type conversions
- Using type casts
- Defining a function that uses an argument

Time Requirements: 1.5 hours

Overview of Contents

In Chapters 3 and 4 we talked about the kinds of data that C recognizes and about data input/output. Now we will look at ways to process the data. C offers many possibilities. We will start with basic arithmetic: addition, subtraction, multiplication, and division. To make our programs more interesting and useful, we will take a first look at loops in this chapter.

6: C CONTROL STATEMENTS: LOOPING

Objectives

- Learning to use C's loop forms: *while*, *for*, and *do while*
- Understanding the difference between entry-condition and exit-condition loops
- Using the relational operators (<, >, >=, <=, !=, and ==) in relational expressions
- Learning the other assignment operators: +=, -=, *=, /=, %=
- Using the comma operator
- Knowing what an array is and how to declare one
- Using the return value for *scanf* to control an input loop
- Defining and using a function with a return value

Time Requirements: 2.5 hours

Overview of Contents

Do you want to create powerful, intelligent, versatile, and useful programs? Then you need a language that provides the three basic forms of program "flow" control. According to computer science (which is the science of computers and not science by computers–yet), a good language should provide these three forms of program flow:

1. Executing a series of statements.
2. Repeating a sequence of statements until some condition is met (called looping).
3. Using a test to decide between alternative actions (called branching).

The first form we know well; all our programs have consisted of a sequence of statements. The *while* loop is one example of the second form. We'll take a closer look at the *while* loop along with two other loop structures: *for* and *do while*. The final form, choosing between different possible courses of action, makes a program much more "intelligent" and increases enormously the usefulness of a computer. You'll have to wait a chapter before being entrusted with such power. But we will look at the varieties of relational expressions and operators that are used both with loop structures and with branching structures. Also, we will talk a bit about arrays, which are often used with loops. Finally, we'll take a first look at functions that return values.

7: C CONTROL STATEMENTS: BRANCHING AND JUMPS

Objectives

- Using the *if* statement to execute statements selectively.
- Using *if else* to choose between two alternatives.
- Using *if else, if...else* or *switch* to choose among multiple alternatives.
- Learning the logical operators: &&, || !
- Using the conditional operator: ?:
- Using the jump commands: *break, continue, goto*
- Using the *getchar* and *putchar* functions.

Time Requirements: 3 hours

Overview of Contents

As you tackle more complex tasks, the flow of your programs becomes more involved. You need programming structures to control and organize these programs. C provides you with valuable tools to meet these needs. You've already learned about looping. In this chapter, we feature branching structures, such as *if* and *switch*, that let you choose alternatives. Also, we look at the logical operators, which let you test for more than one relationship in a *while* or *if* condition. And we look at C's jump statements, which shift the program flow to another part of a program.

8: CHARACTER INPUT/OUTPUT

8.1 *Single-Character I/O*
8.2 *Buffers*
8.3 *Terminating Keyboard Input*
8.4 *Redirection and Files*
8.5 *A Graphic Example*
8.6 *Creating a More Friendly User Interface*
8.7 *Menu Browsing*
8.8 *Summary*

Objectives

- Learning the difference between buffered and unbuffered input
- Understanding how C treats I/O devices as files
- Learning how to detect the end of a file
- Learning how to simulate end of file from the keyboard
- Using input and output redirection
- Learning how to better handle input
- Checking input for validity

Time Requirements: 2 hours

Overview of Contents

The words "input" and "output" have more than one use in computing. We can talk about input and output devices, such as keyboards, disk drives, and dot matrix printers. Or we can talk about the data that are used for input and output. And we can talk about the functions that perform input and output. Our main intent in this chapter is to discuss functions used for input and output (I/O for short).

By I/O functions we mean functions that transport data to and from your program. We've used several such functions already: *printf*, *scanf*, *getchar*, and *putchar*. In this chapter we'll take a closer look at the conceptual basis for these functions. Also, we'll see how to improve the program-user interface.

Input/output functions originally were not part of the definition of C; their development was left to the implementors of C. In practice, the Unix implementation of C has served as a model for these functions. The ANSI C standard library, recognizing past practice, contains a large number of these I/O functions, including the ones we've used. Such standard functions must work in a wide variety of computer environments, so they don't take advantage of features peculiar to a particular system. Thus many C implementors supply additional I/O functions that do make use of special features, such as the 8086 microprocessor I/O ports. These functions let you write programs that utilize a particular computer more effectively, but often they can't be used on other computer systems. We'll concentrate on the standard I/O functions available on all systems, for they allow you to write portable programs that can be moved easily from one system to another.

9: FUNCTIONS

Objectives

- Learning to define a function
- Using arguments to communicate values from the calling function to the called function
- Understanding the difference between a formal argument and an actual argument
- Knowing where to declare arguments and where to declare the other local variables in a function
- Using *return* to communicate a value from the called program to the calling program
- Learning when and how to use addresses and pointers for communication
- Understanding function types and knowing when and where to declare functions

- Using ANSI C function prototyping
- Knowing when to use the *void* type

Time Requirements: 2.5 hours

Overview of Contents

The design philosophy of C is based on using functions. Already we have used several functions to help our programming: *printf*, *scanf*, *getchar*, *putchar*, and *strlen*. These functions come with the system, but we also created several functions of our own. Most of them have been called *main*, for programs always start by executing the instructions in *main*; after that, *main* can call other functions, like *printf* or ones of our own design, into action. We've already previewed several aspects of creating your own functions. In this chapter we'll consolidate that information and expand upon it. Also, we'll look at the new ANSI C methods for defining and using functions.

10: ARRAYS AND POINTERS

Objectives

- Declaring a one-dimensional array.
- Initializing a one-dimensional array.
- Previewing external and static storage classes.
- Getting the address of a variable.
- Learning about pointers.

- Using the indirection operator to access the value a pointer points to.
- Using array names as pointers.
- Learning array-pointer correspondences.
- Knowing the five operations you can apply to pointer variables.
- Using pointers in functions operating on arrays.
- Declaring a two-dimensional array.
- Writing functions to process two-dimensional arrays.

Time Requirements: 3.5 hours

Overview of Contents

Arrays and pointers have an intimate relationship to each other, so traditionally they are discussed together. Before we explore that relationship, however, we will review and augment our knowledge of arrays. Then we will study the connection with pointers.

11: CHARACTER STRINGS AND STRING FUNCTIONS

Objectives

- Declaring character arrays
- Initializing character arrays
- Creating string constants
- Initializing pointers to strings
- Creating arrays of strings
- Using *gets* and *puts* for string I/O
- Using string functions from the C library
- Using character functions from the C library
- Using command-line arguments
- Converting strings to numbers

Time Requirements: 3.5 hours

Overview of Contents

Character strings form one of the most useful and important data types in C. Although we have been using character strings all along, we still have much to learn about them. Of course, we already know the most basic fact: a character string is a *char* array terminated with a null character (\0). In this chapter we will learn more about the nature of strings, how to declare and initialize strings, how to get them into and out of programs, and how to manipulate strings.

12: FILE INPUT/OUTPUT

12.1 *Communicating with Files*
12.2 *Low-Level I/O*
12.3 *Standard I/O*
12.4 *A Simple File-Condensing Program*
12.5 *File I/O: More Functions*
12.6 *Random Access:* fseek *and* ftell
12.7 *Behind the Scenes with Standard I/O*
12.8 *Other Standard I/O Functions*
12.9 *Summary/Review*

Objectives

- Knowing what a file is
- Understanding text modes and binary modes
- Using low-level I/O services
- Buffered and non-buffered I/O
- Using the standard I/O library
- Knowing the advantages of the standard I/O library
- Using random access in a file
- Understanding text and binary data formats

Time Requirements: 2 hours

Overview of Contents

In Chapter 8 you learned simple character I/O using the keyboard and screen. The keyboard and screen are actually files–called "standard input" (*stdin*) and "standard output" (*stdout*). Now we move on to look at files in general and how your program can create and use them. As a programmer, you may have to write programs that create files, write into files, and read from files. We'll investigate two levels of file communications: low-level I/O and stream I/O.

13: STORAGE CLASSES AND PROGRAM DEVELOPMENT

Objectives

- Understanding automatic, external, static, and register storage classes
- Knowing the scope and duration of variables
- Understanding the difference between defining declarations and referencing declarations
- Learning about the type qualifiers *const* and *volatile*
- Thinking of a function as a black box with information flow
- Using data verification

Time Requirements: 2 hours

Overview of Contents

One of C's strengths is that it lets you control the fine points of a program. C's storage classes are an example of that control because they allow you to determine which functions know which variables and how long a variable persists in a program. Storage classes form the first topic of this chapter.

A second topic is that there is more to programming than just knowing the rules of the language, just as there is more to writing a novel (or even a letter) than knowing the rules of English. We will reinforce some of the general principles and concepts of program design that we've introduced earlier. We will also develop several useful functions. As we do so, we will try to demonstrate some of the considerations that go into the designing of a function. In particular, we will emphasize the value of a modular approach, the breaking down of jobs into manageable tasks.

14: STRUCTURES

Objectives

- Defining a structure template
- Creating structure variables
- Using structure tags
- Accessing structure members
- Using pointers to structures to access structure members
- Defining and using nested structures
- Defining and using arrays of structures

Time Requirements: 1.25 hours

Overview of Contents

Often the success of a program depends on finding a good way to represent the data with which the program must work. C, through design, has a very powerful means to represent complex data. This data form, called a structure, not only is flexible enough in its basic form to represent a diversity of data, but also allows the user to invent new forms. If you are familiar with the "records" of Pascal, you should be comfortable with structures.

15: C PREPROCESSOR/C LIBRARY

Objectives

- Defining symbolic constants
- Defining macro functions
- Understanding the advantages and disadvantages of macros
- Including files
- Using the C library
- Using math functions

Time Requirements: .5 hours

Overview of Contents

This chapter examines the C preprocessor and the C library. The preprocessor is used to tell the compiler to work in special ways, to ignore certain sections of source code, or to compile sections based on the condition of a flag character at the beginning of the source code. You'll learn how to use preprocessor symbolic constants, how to define and use macro functions that save you a great deal of typing, and what "include" files are. Details about the powerful and large C library are also covered in this chapter, and examples of how to use the math functions in the C library are provided. A more extensive treatment of the C library can be found in the The Waite Group's C Bibles. (Note that this chapter differs from Chapter 15 in *The Waite Group's New C Primer Plus,* which covers bit fiddling).

Chapter 6 ➤ IN CASE OF TROUBLE

Master C has been thoroughly tested in a number of machine environments. While there should be very few problems, one problem you might encounter concerns the screen device driver. Master C uses a device driver to control output to the screen. If you see a host of strange characters displayed immediately after the logo screen, the device driver has not been loaded.

NANSI.SYS

Your package comes with NANSI.SYS, and this will be copied to your hard disk by the install program. A reference to this driver will also be included in your CONFIG.SYS file. To correct the strange character problem you may only have to restart your computer, since device drivers are loaded into the computer from the hard disk *only* when the computer is first started.

If the problem persists after restarting the computer, you may have to adjust your CONFIG.SYS file directly. Or you may have another device driver which is in conflict. Use your editor to check CONFIG.SYS. Ensure that the following line is included:

DEVICE = NANSI.SYS or DEVICE = ANSI.SYS

Of course, there will be many other lines of code in the CONFIG.SYS file, all of which should be left unaltered. Save the file and try restarting the computer again.

Color vs Monochrome

Master C assumes you have a color display (CGA or EGA) connected to your computer. However, some IBM PC compatible computers use amber, gray, or green monochrome displays. Because Master C uses colors that may be incompatible with certain monochome displays, you may find that Master C will not initially display bright and non-bright characters properly. If you find your text screen is difficult to read it can be corrected by simply switching Master C to the monochome display mode. To do this first press the **H** key to enable the Help window. When the Help window is open, press the **C** key. This will change the Master C Color Map from color to monochrome. Your text should now be easy to read.

Disk Errors

If, when installing Master C, you get a disk error try starting the install process over. Disk errors are almost always caused by a difference in drive alignments. If reinstalling fails, try copying the disks one at a time to a second floppy disk drive. If this doesn't work try copying the disks one at a time on a different computer system. Often one computer will read disks that are slightly out of alignment and the process of rewriting them to a floppy will produce a copy that will be less out of alignment than the originals.

Master C Incompatibilities

Master C will NOT work with any version of DOS 2 or lower. Only DOS 3 and up are compatible with Master C.

Master C will not work with an IBM 3270 terminal or an IBM 3270 terminal emulator.

Chapter 7 ➤ TIPS, TECHNIQUES, & WHAT'S NEXT

Here are a collection of tips and tricks that might help you learn Master C more effectively.

Using Master C

➤ If you have a printer you can study a Master C screen away from the computer by using the print screen command of DOS to capture the screen to paper. On an old-style PC Keyboard *Shift-PrtSc* are the keys to press to cause the Master C screen to be printed. On a newer AT-style keyboard use the *Print Screen* key to capture a screen to paper. Some users like to build their own personal book of C this way.

➤ To reset the achievement scores you must delete the files in the directory C:\MASTERC\REGISTER and restart Master C. This technique is necessary since Master C is to be used like a book—one person uses it at a time: Master C is only licensed to one user (the original purchaser). For multiple users a PC network version of Master C is available from The Waite Group. Please write or call for details.

Installing Master C

➤ You can copy all of the files from each of the four 5.25 inch disks one at a time to four 3.5 inch disks, then install them on your computer.

➤ Note that the installation process is very slow on older PC's because they have such low clock speed (4.77 MHz). The installation on an older PC can be up to an hour. Installation on a PC AT will only take about 15 minutes and on a 386 it will be under 10 minutes.

➤ When you install Master C a second time on the hard disk and use the original directory you used for the first installation (MASTERC is the default) the installation routine will report that it was unable to create a directory at the end of the installation steps. You can ignore this warning message.

➤ It is possible to install Master C on the menu system of QuickC. This allows you to call Master C from QuickC with the mouse. When you are done you can quit Master C and you will be automatically returned to the QuickC environment. Consult your QuickC documentation for details on how this is done.

What's Next?

While using Master C, you are probably anxious to start writing and running your own C programs. To do so you need a C compiler. Sooner or later you will probably want to add some books on C to your library—and you may have noticed that the bookstore shelves are packed to bursting with books on virtually all flavors of C and aspects of C programming.

Therefore we will just mention a few titles that we have found to be complimentary to Master C and helpful.

IBM PC and Compatible Tutorials

In the PC-compatible world both Microsoft with *QuickC*, and Borland with *Turbo C*, provide inexpensive, easy to use, and surprisingly powerful C compilers. (Microsoft also provides a more expensive professional developer version of C called Microsoft C 6.0).

All of these products integrate an editor, compiler, linker, and other features into a single menu-driven package—you write your program using the built-in editor and then compile and run the program with a single keystroke. These products also feature powerful built-in debuggers and extensive context-sensitive online help. The professional development C 6.0 from Microsoft provides additional debugging and programmer related tools, including the ability to compile code for OS/2.

If you choose QuickC, a good way to get up to speed is to work through *The Waite Group's Microsoft QuickC Programming, Second Edition* by Mitchell Waite, Stephen Prata, Byran Costales, and Harry Henderson. (Microsoft Press, Redmond, WA, 1990.)

A good primer for Turbo C (including details on the new Turbo C++ compiler) is *The Waite Group's C Programming Using Turbo C++*, by Robert Lafore (Howard W. Sams & Company, Carmel, IN, 1990).

For a good tutorial on Microsoft C 6.0, examine *The Waite Group's Microsoft C Programming for the PC, Second Edition*, by Robert Lafore (Howard W. Sams & Company, Carmel, IN, 1990).

These books are also good once you have perfected your basic C skills since you can turn to mastering the intricacies of the PC's hardware—drawing screen graphics, reading special keys on the keyboard, and calling upon DOS and BIOS services.

Generic C Tutorial

Any of these books will help you familiarize yourself with a compiler for the IBM PC. However, if you work with the UNIX operating system or another non-PC operating system, or if you are interested in a more traditional, non-operating system dependent approach to learning C, you will want to see *C: Step by Step* by Mitchell Waite and Stephen Prata (Howard W. Sams & Company, Carmel, IN, 1989). This book was designed with the classroom environment in mind and was put together using a committee of college professors. It is similar to *The Waite Group's New C Primer Plus* and, except for Chapters 15 and 16, the heading numbers correspond to the menu numbers in Master C.

C Library Reference Books

The Microsoft and Borland C compilers come with hundreds of library functions, many dealing with specific applications and the need to interface with the operating system, ROM BIOS, and hardware devices. Working with these extensive, powerful libraries is easier if you have a good desktop reference at hand. *The Waite Group's Microsoft C Bible, Second Edition,* by Naba Barkakati (Howard W. Sams & Company, Carmel, IN, 1990) serves as a comprehensive, example-filled reference that includes tutorial overviews of the language, compiler, and specific areas of the library. The companion book for Turbo C is *The Waite Group's Turbo C Bible,* by Naba Barkakati (Howard W. Sams & Company, Carmel, IN, 1989.) There is also a Turbo C++ version of this book called *The Waite Group's Turbo C++ Bible,* by Naba Barkakati (Howard W. Sams & Company, Carmel, IN, 1990.)

For All C Programmers

All C programmers should have a copy of *The C Programming Language, Second Edition,* by Brian W. Kernighan and Dennis M. Ritchie, (Prentice Hall, Englewood Cliffs, NJ, 1988). This is virtually the official definition and specification for ANSI C, laying out all of the nuances of the language's grammar.

Magazines

C Users Journal

To keep up on the latest developments in the C language you might want to subscribe to the *C Users Journal.* The magazine has lots of good columnists, several on the ANSI C and C++ committees. The articles are fairly high level.

C Users Journal , 2601 Iowa Street, Lawrence, KS 66047 USA (913) 841-1631 (voice), (913) 841-2624 (FAX). 1 yr $28 (12 issues), 2 yrs $52 (24 issues), 3 yrs $75 (36 issues).

PC Techniques

This is a new magazine run by a former editor of Dr. Dobbs, and a prolific and popular author, Jeff Duntemann, and Keith Weiskamp, another prolific author and industry mogul. The magazine takes the place of *PC Tech Journal,* a once popular but now defunct magazine formerly published by Ziff Davis. *PC Techniques* has a nice blend of articles on programing in C and C++, as well as Turbo Pascal. The level is perfect for someone learning C for the first time, or wanting to continue to expand their understanding of the language. Unlike other magazines, *PC Techniques* publishes book reviews.

PC Techniques, A Coriolis Group Publication, 3202 E. Greenway, Suite 1307-302, Phoenix, AZ, 85032, (602) 483-0192. 1 yr $21.95 (7 issues), 2 yrs $37.95 (13 issues).

As a C programmer you have a varied and interesting journey ahead of you. We wish you good travelling.

II Master C Reference

Chapter 8 ➤ REFERENCE OVERVIEW

The printed reference materials for Master C are divided into two major parts: Chapter 8—a reference overview and Chapter 9—a detailed alphabetical listing. This chapter briefly introduces each of the elements of C that are covered in the detailed reference. The following elements are covered:

- language keywords, such as *char* and *while*
- operators, such as + and *sizeof*
- preprocessor directives, such as *#include* and *#define*
- predefined values, such as *_DATE_* and *BUFSIZ*
- predefined data types, such as *time_t* and *va_list*
- character escape sequences, such as *\n* and *\t*
- library functions, such as *fopen* and *printf*

This overview presents groups of related items and a summary of their use. Since mastering the use of the ANSI library functions is particularly important, the overview divides them into ten functionally-related groups (such as Streams and Files, Process Control, and Data Conversion). Most groups of functions are presented with two tables: one that lists the functions in the group alphabetically, and one that divides them according to the task performed, such as opening a file, reading data from a file, and writing data to a file.

The bulk of the reference is the alphabetical list in Chapter 9. If you are interested in a particular keyword, function, macro, data structure, or other item, you can go directly to its entry and see a description of the item's purpose and a summary and often an example of its use. Before using the alphabetical list for the first time, please read the note on using of the reference that precedes it.

ANSI C AND BEYOND

Master C is based on the ANSI standard for C, adopted in 1989, which provides a "portable" core of language elements and functions. Programs that use only ANSI-defined elements should run on any ANSI-compliant compiler regardless of the hardware involved, though the reference entries note that some items (such as the size of data types) are system-dependent or implementation-dependent. The overview and alphabetical reference sections cover only ANSI-defined keywords, predefined values, and functions.

Most real-world C compilers supplement the ANSI-compliant elements with hundreds of additional functions and a variety of special features. The ANSI standard doesn't include any graphics functions, for example, because graphics are highly hardware dependent. If you will be working with the Microsoft or Borland C compilers for the IBM PC, we recommend the following "bibles" from The Waite Group and Howard W. Sams:

The Waite Group's Microsoft C Bible. Second Edition. Howard W. Sams, Carmel, IN: 1990.

The Waite Group's Turbo C^{++} Bible. Howard W. Sams, Carmel, IN: 1990.

These books provide introductory tutorials on the C language and a detailed reference section for each of the categories of library functions, including complete example programs.

OVERVIEW OF LANGUAGE ELEMENTS

We can now look at each of the kinds of items that make up the C language and environment, and that are covered in the alphabetical reference.

ANSI KEYWORDS

ANSI keywords are used to provide control structures (such as *if* and *while*), data types (such as *char* and *float*) and qualifying terms that specify how data types or variables will be handled (such as *unsigned* and *volatile*). Keywords are also sometimes called "reserved words" because they are reserved for the use of the compiler—you can't use them as variable names. It is, however, all right to embed a keyword in a variable name—for example, *charptr.* Table 1 lists the ANSI C keywords, each of which has its own entry in the alphabetic reference.

Table 1. ANSI C Keywords

auto	double	int	struct
break	else	long	switch
case	enum	register	typedef
char	extern	return	union
const	float	short	unsigned
continue	for	signed	void
default	goto	sizeof	volatile
do	if	static	while

OPERATORS AND PRECEDENCE

Operators are language elements that manipulate variables or data in some way, such as by adding data items together, getting the address of a variable, comparing the size of two numbers, and so on. Each operator has an entry in the alphabetical reference. Because all of the operators except *sizeof* and the type cast *(<type>)* consist of non-alphabetic characters, we have placed all the operators in the reference chapter in a sequence that *precedes* the letter a.

Table 2 lists all of the ANSI C operators, grouped by category.

An important consideration in using operators is the precedence, or order in which operators take effect. Within a given level of prece-

Table 2. Operators in C.

<table>
<tr><th>Operator</th><th>Name</th><th>Example</th><th>Explanation</th></tr>
<tr><td colspan="4">ARITHMETIC OPERATORS</td></tr>
<tr><td>*</td><td>Multiplication</td><td>x*y</td><td>Multiply x and y</td></tr>
<tr><td>/</td><td>Division</td><td>x/y</td><td>Divide x by y</td></tr>
<tr><td>%</td><td>Modulo</td><td>x%y</td><td>Remainder of x divided by y</td></tr>
<tr><td>+</td><td>Addition</td><td>x+y</td><td>Add x and y</td></tr>
<tr><td>–</td><td>Subtraction</td><td>x–y</td><td>Subtract y from x</td></tr>
<tr><td>++</td><td>Increment</td><td>x++</td><td>Increment x after use</td></tr>
<tr><td>––</td><td>Decrement</td><td>––x</td><td>Decrement x before use</td></tr>
<tr><td>–</td><td>Negation</td><td>–x</td><td>Negate the value of x</td></tr>
<tr><td>+</td><td>Unary Plus</td><td>+x</td><td>Value of x (new in ANSI C)</td></tr>
<tr><td colspan="4">RELATIONAL AND LOGICAL OPERATORS</td></tr>
<tr><td>></td><td>Greater than</td><td>x>y</td><td>1 if x exceeds y, else 0</td></tr>
<tr><td>>=</td><td>Greater than or equal to</td><td>x>=y</td><td>1 if x is greater than or equal to y, else 0</td></tr>
<tr><td><</td><td>Less than</td><td>x<y</td><td>1 if y exceeds x, else 0</td></tr>
<tr><td><=</td><td>Less than or equal to</td><td>x<=y</td><td>1 if x is less than or equal to y, else 0</td></tr>
<tr><td>==</td><td>Equal to</td><td>x==y</td><td>1 if x equals y, else 0</td></tr>
<tr><td>!=</td><td>Not equal to</td><td>x!=y</td><td>1 if x and y unequal, else 0</td></tr>
<tr><td>!</td><td>Logical NOT</td><td>!x</td><td>1 if x is 0, else 0</td></tr>
<tr><td>&&</td><td>Logical AND</td><td>x&&y</td><td>0 if either x or y is 0</td></tr>
<tr><td>||</td><td>Logical OR</td><td>x||y</td><td>0 if both x and y are 0</td></tr>
</table>

(continued)

Table 2 *(continued)*

Operator	Name	Example	Explanation
ASSIGNMENT OPERATORS			
=	Assignment	x=y;	put value of y into x
0=	Compound assignment	x 0= y;	equivalent to x = x 0 y; assignment where 0 is one of the operators: + – * / % << >> & ^ |
DATA ACCESS AND SIZE OPERATORS			
[ ]	Array element	x[0]	first element of array x
.	Member selection	s.x	member x in structure s
->	Member selection	p->x	member named x in a structure that p points to
*	Indirection	*p	contents of location whose address is in p
&	Address of	&x	address of x
sizeof	Size in bytes	sizeof(x)	size of x in bytes
BITWISE OPERATORS			
~	Bitwise complement	~x	flip 1 bits to 0 and complement 0 bits to 1
&	Bitwise AND	x&y	bitwise AND of x and y
|	Bitwise OR	x|y	bitwise OR of x and y
^	Bitwise exclusive OR	x^y	value with 1's at bits where corresponding bits of x and y differ
<<	Left shift	x << 4	x shifted to the left by 4 bit positions
>>	Right shift	x >> 4	x shifted to the right by 4 bit positions
MISCELLANEOUS OPERATORS			
()	Function	malloc(10)	call malloc with argument 10
(type)	Type cast	(double)i	i converted to a double
? :	Conditional	x1 ? x2 : x3	if x1 is not 0, x2 is evaluated, else x3 is evaluated
,	Sequential evaluation	i++, m++	first increment i, then increment m

dence the order in which operators take effect is called "associativity." Table 3 gives both the precedence and associativity of all of the ANSI C operators.

Table 3. Operator Precedence and Associativity in C

Operator type	Operators	Associativity
Expression	() [] . ->	Left to right
Unary	– + ~ ! * & ++ – – sizeof (type)	Right to left
Multiplicative	* / %	Left to right
Additive	+ –	Left to right
Shift	<< >>	Left to right
Relational (inequality)	< <= > >=	Left to right
Relational (equality)	== !=	Left to right
Bitwise AND	&	Left to right
Bitwise XOR	^	Left to right
Bitwise OR	|	Left to right
Logical AND	&&	Left to right
Logical OR	| |	Left to right
Conditional	? :	Right to left
Assignment	= *= /= %= += –= <<= >>= &= |= ^=	Right to left
Sequential Evaluation	,	Left to right

Thus the expression $a * b / c + d$ is evaluated by doing multiplication and division first, since they have a higher precedence than addition. Because the associativity for the multiplicative operators is from left to right, $a * b$ is performed first, then the result is divided by c. Finally d is added to the result. Of course you can use parentheses to override precedence: in the expression $(a * b) / (c + d)$ the multiplication and addition in parentheses are peformed first, and then the division.

PREPROCESSOR DIRECTIVES AND MACROS

The preprocessor processes the source text of a program file and acts on commands, called "preprocessor directives," embedded in the text. These directives begin with the character #. Usually the compiler automatically invokes the preprocessor before beginning compilation, but most compilers will allow you to invoke the preprocessor alone by using compiler options. The preprocessor provides three important services that enable users to make their programs modular, more easily readable, and easier to customize for different computer systems. The services are: including the contents of a file into a C program (file inclusion); replacing one string with another (token replacement and macro processing); and compiling selected portions of a program (conditional compilation). Table 4 summarizes the preprocessor directives. Each preprocessor directive also has an entry in the alphabetical reference.

Table 4. ANSI C Preprocessor Directives

Directive	Meaning
# operator	String-izing operator
Example:	#define show(x) printf(#x) show(me); expands to printf("me");
## operator	Token-pasting operator
Example:	#define version(x) MSC##x version(5) results in the token MSC5
#define	Define a symbol or a macro (you can redefine a macro with the same expression as often as you want)
Example:	#define double(x) ((x)+(x)) r=double(2.0); sets r to 4.0
#elif	Else if operator (see example for #if)
#else	Else operator (see example for #if)
#endif	Mark the end of an #if directive
#error	Produce diagnostic message
Example:	#if defined(WRONG_OPTION) #error Recompile with correct option #endif
#if	Conditional directive
Example:	#if !defined(FILE_1_INCLUDED) #include <file1.h> #elif defined(INCLUDE_FILE_2)

(continued)

Table 4 *(continued)*

Directive	Meaning
	#include <file2.h>
	#else
	#include <file3.h>
	#endif
#ifdef	Equivalent to #if defined
#ifndef	Equivalent to #if !defined
#include	File inclusion
Example:	#include <stdio.h>
#line	Set the current line number
#pragma	Instruct the compiler
#undef	Remove the definition of a symbol

The ANSI C standard requires a number of preprocessor symbols to be predefined by the compiler. Table 5 lists these macros. Note that all such predefined macros must start with a leading underscore (_) followed by a capital letter or another underscore. You can not use *#undef* to remove the definitions of these macros. Each of these macros also has an entry in the alphabetical reference.

Table 5. ANSI C Predefined Macros

Macro Name	Defined to be
DATE	The date of translation of the source file in the form of a string of the form "MMM DD YYYY" (such as "Jul 12 1988")
FILE	A string containing the name of the source file
LINE	The line number of the current source file, as a decimal constant
STDC	The decimal constant 1 to indicate that the C compiler conforms to the ANSI standard
TIME	The time of translation of the source file as a string of the form "HH:MM:SS"

OTHER PREDEFINED VALUES AND DATA TYPES

ANSI C provides predefined values that allow the programmer to access implementation-dependent values, such as the minimum and maximum sizes for various character and numeric data types, the locale (national format) in use, and so on. There are also many data types defined in the header files for use by various library functions, such as file information, time, and date formats. All of these values have individual entries in the alphabetical reference.

ESCAPE SEQUENCES

Escape sequences allow you to include special characters such as a newline or tab in strings. A backslash (\) introduces each escape sequence. Table 6 lists the escape sequences supported by ANSI C. Note that you can specify any character in your machine's character set by following the backslash with the octal (base 8) character code, or with an *x* followed by the hexadecimal character code.

Table 6. ANSI Character Escape Sequences

Sequence	Name	Meaning when printed
\a	alert	Produce an audible alert.
\b	backspace	Move character position backwards.
\f	form feed	Move to the beginning of a new page.
\n	new-line	Move to beginning of next line.
\r	carriage return	Move to beginning of current line.
\t	horizontal tab	Move to next tabulation position on this line.
\v	vertical tab	Move to next vertical tabulation point.
\\		Interpret as a single backslash.
\'		Interpret as '
\"		Interpret as "
\?		Interpret as ?
\<octal digits>		Interpretation depends on printer or terminal
\x<hexadecimal digits>		Interpretation depends on printer or terminal

FUNCTIONS AND THE ANSI LIBRARY

Functions are the building blocks of C programs. They are independent collections of declarations and statements you mix and match to create stand-alone applications. Each C program has at least one function: the *main* function. The library specified in ANSI C consists mostly of functions (in addition to quite a few macros). For the most part, developing software in C involves writing functions.

Fortunately, C compilers provide a large variety of already written and compiled functions in libraries. The declarations for these functions, and for certain constants and data types that they use, are provided in *header* files. Table 7 lists the header files that are required by the ANSI standard. Many compilers provide additional ones for graphics, calls to operating system functions, and other hardware-dependent matters.

Table 7. Standard Header Files in ANSI C

Header file name	Description
assert.h	Defines the *assert* macro and NDEBUG symbol. Used for program diagnostics.
ctype.h	Declares character classification and conversion routines.
errno.h	Defines macros for error conditions, EDOM and ERANGE, and the integer variable *errno*.
float.h	Defines symbols for the maximum and minimum values of floating-point numbers.
limits.h	Defines symbols for the limiting values of all integer data types.
locale.h	Declares functions necessary for customizing a C program to a particular locale. Defines the *lconv* structure.
math.h	Declares the math functions and the HUGE_VAL constant.
setjmp.h	Defines the *jmp_buf* data type used by the routines *setjmp* and *longjmp*.
signal.h	Defines symbols and routines necessary for handling exceptional conditions.
stdarg.h	Defines the macros that facilitate handling variable-length argument lists.
stddef.h	Defines the standard data types *ptrdiff_t, size_t, wchar_t,* the symbol *NULL,* and the macro offsetof.

(continued)

Table 7 *(continued)*

Header file name	Description
stdlib.h	Declares the utility functions such as the string conversion routines, random number generator, memory allocation routines, and process control routines.
string.h	Declares the string manipulation routines.
time.h	Defines data type *time_t*, the *tm* data structure, and declares the *time* functions.

The following sections present the library functions in ten categories. For each category two tables—one alphabetical and one organized by task—give you an overview of each set of related functions.

STREAMS AND FILES

The C programming language has no built-in capability to perform any input and output (I/O). This task is the responsibility of the library accompanying your C compiler. Fortunately, the ANSI standard for C also specifies the I/O functions which must be present in a standard-conforming compiler. Table 8 lists all the I/O routines alphabetically, and Table 9 groups them by task.

Table 8. Alphabetical List of ANSI C File I/O Routines

Name of Routine	Description
clearerr	Clears the error indicator of a stream.
fclose	Closes a stream.
feof	A macro that returns a non-zero value if current position in a stream is at the end of file.
ferror	A macro that returns a non-zero value if an error had occurred during read/write operations on a stream.
fflush	Writes to the file the contents of the buffer associated with a stream.
fgetc	Reads a character from a stream.
fgetpos	Returns current position of a stream in an internal format suitable for use by fsetpos.
fgets	Reads a line (up to and including the first newline character) from a stream.
fopen	Opens a named file as a buffered stream (includes options for selecting translation modes and access types).
fprintf	Performs formatted output to a stream.

(continued)

Table 8 *(continued)*

Name of Routine	Description
fputc	Writes a character to a stream.
fputs	Writes a string of characters to a stream.
fread	Reads a specified amount of binary data from a stream.
freopen	Closes a stream and reassigns it to a new file.
fscanf	Performs formatted input from a stream.
fseek	Sets current position to a specific location in the file.
fsetpos	Sets current position of a stream using value returned by an earlier call to fgetpos.
ftell	Returns the current position in the file associated with a stream.
fwrite	Writes a specified number of bytes of binary data to a stream.
getc	Reads a character from a stream.
getchar	Reads a character from the stream stdin.
gets	Reads a string upto a newline character from the stream stdin.
printf	Performs formatted output to the stream stdout.
putc	Writes a character to a stream.
putchar	Writes a character to the stream stdout.
puts	Writes a C string to the stream stdout.
remove	Deletes a file specifed by its name.
rename	Changes the name of a file to a new one.
rewind	Sets the current position to the beginning of the file associated with a stream.
scanf	Performs formatted input from the stream stdin.
setbuf	Assigns a fixed-length user-defined buffer to an open stream.
setvbuf	Assigns a variable-length user-defined buffer to an open stream.
sprintf	Performs formatted output to a buffer.
sscanf	Performs formatted input from a buffer.
tmpfile	Creates a temprary file open for buffered stream I/O.
tmpnam	Generates a temporary file name.
ungetc	Pushes a character back into the buffer associated with a stream.
vfprintf	Version of fprintf that accepts a pointer to a list of arguments and performs formatted output to a stream.
vprintf	Version of printf that accepts a pointer to a list of arguments and performs formatted output to the stream stdout.
vsprintf	Version of sprintf that accepts a pointer to a list of arguments and performs formatted output to a buffer.

Table 9. File I/O Routines in ANSI C Classified by Task

I/O Task	Routine name
Create or open a file	fopen, freopen
Close a file	fclose
Delete or rename a file	remove, rename
Formatted read	fscanf, scanf
Formatted write	fprintf, printf, vfprintf, vprintf
Read a character	fgetc, fgetchar, getc, getchar
Write a character	fputc, fputchar, putc, putchar
Read a line	fgets, gets
Write a line	fputs, puts
Set read/write position	fseek, fsetpos, rewind
Get read/write position	fgetpos, ftell
Binary read	fread
Binary write	fwrite
Flush buffer	fflush
Check error/eof	clearerr, feof, ferror
Manage temporary files	tmpfile, tmpnam
Control buffering	setbuf, setvbuf
Push character to buffer	ungetc

PROCESS CONTROL AND LOCALE ROUTINES

The process control routines include the signal handling functions that take care of error conditions, and utility functions to terminate a process, communicate with the operating system, and set up numeric and currency formats depending on the locale for which your program is customized. These routines are defined in locale.h, signal.h, setjmp.h, and stdlib.h. Table 10 lists these routines alphabetically, and Table 11 groups them by task.

Table 10. Alphabetical List of ANSI C Process Control and Locale Routines

Name of Routine	Description
abort	Raises the SIGABRT signal after printing a message to stderr. The normal handler for SIGABRT terminates the process without flushing file buffers.
assert	Prints a diagnostic message and aborts program, if a given logical expression is false.
atexit	Installs a routine to a stack of at least 32 routines that will be called in "last-in first-out" order when the process terminates.
exit	Calls the functions installed by atexit, flushes all buffers associated with streams that are open for I/O, and finally terminates the process and returns to the operating system.
getenv	Returns the definition of an environment variable from the envrionment of the process.
localeconv	Sets the componets of a lconv structure with information about numeric and monetary formatting appropriate for the current locale.
longjmp	Restores the context of a process thus affecting an unconditional jump to the place where setjmp was called to save that particular context.
perror	Prints an error message using your message and the system message corresponding to the value in the global variable errno.
raise	Generates a signal (an exception).
setjmp	Saves the context of a process in a buffer that can be used by longjmp to jump back.
signal	Installs a function to handle a specific exception or signal.
setlocale	Selects a locale for a specified portion of the program's locale-dependent aspects.
system	Executes an operating system command.

Table 11. ANSI C Process Control and Locale Routines by Task

Task	Name of Routines
Execute an operating system command	system
Terminate a process	abort, exit
Handle errors	assert, perror
Get environment	getenv
Install exception handler and generate an exception	raise, signal

(continued)

Table 11 *(continued)*

Task	Name of Routines
Non-local jump from from one function to another	longjmp, setjmp
Install routines to be called when the process terminates	atexit
Control locale-specific numeric and currency formatting	localeconv, setlocale

VARIABLE ARGUMENT LIST ROUTINES

In writing C programs, you encounter built-in functions such as *printf* that can take a variable number of arguments. Sometimes it is convenient to custom write your own routines that can process a variable number of arguments. Take, for instance, a routine (*findmax*) that picks the largest element from an array of integers. If the routine can accept a variable number of arguments, you can use such calls as *findmax(1,2,3)* and *findmax(a,b,c,d)* to find the maximum of any number of arguments. A set of macros in ANSI C makes a straightforward task of handling a variable number of arguments. Table 12 lists the variable argument handling routines alphabetically—since there are only three of them, no task-oriented table is given.

Table 12. Alphabetical List of Variable Argument Macros

Name of Macro	Description
va_arg	Gets the next argument from the stack.
va_end	Resets everything so that the function can return normally.
va_start	Initializes the argument pointer to the address of the first argument to the function.

ANSI C MEMORY ALLOCATION ROUTINES

Most computer systems store instructions and data in memory and use a central processing unit (CPU) such as the Intel 80x86 microprocessor in an IBM PC or the Motorola 680x0 in an Apple Macintosh to repeatedly retrieve instructions from memory and execute them. The operating system, itself a program residing in memory, takes care of loading other programs and executing them. The operating system has its own scheme of managing the available memory for its data and that for other programs as well.

In older programming languages, such as FORTRAN, there is no provision for requesting memory at run-time. All data items and arrays have to be declared before compiling the program. You have to guess beforehand the maximum size of an array and there is no way to exceed the maximum other than recompiling the program. This is inefficient because you are locking in the maximum amount of memory your program will ever need.

In most modern languages, including C, you can request blocks of memory at run-time and release the blocks when your program no longer needs them. A major advantage of this capability is that you can design your application to exploit all available memory in the system. Like most other capabilities in C, this capability comes in the form of a set of library routines, known as the memory allocation routines. The specific set that comes with ANSI C has four basic memory allocation routines, cataloged in Table 13. (Again, due to the limited number of routines in this category, there is no task-oriented table.)

Table 13. Alphabetical List of ANSI C Memory Allocation Routines

Name of Routine	Description
calloc	Allocates memory for an array of data elements and initializes them to zero.
free	Frees previously allocated memory.
malloc	Allocates a number of bytes and returns a pointer to the first byte of the allocated memory.
realloc	Enlarges or shrinks a previously allocated block of memory moving the block in the physical memory of the system, if necessary.

ANSI C DATA CONVERSION ROUTINES

INTRODUCTION

Information management with computers frequently requires crunching numbers. These numbers are internally represented in several forms depending on the type of C variable in which the value is held. It is more convenient to have users enter numbers as strings, however, since strings can be scanned and otherwise checked using a variety of routines. The ANSI C data conversion routines, declared in the header file stdlib.h, allow converting strings to the internal forms needed by numeric variables. These routines are listed alphabetically in Table 14 and by task in Table 15.

Note that there are a few additional routines in the C library which also provide data conversion facilities. The *sprintf* and the *sscanf* functions in the I/O category can respectively convert internal values to strings and strings back to internal representations. The *sscanf* routine, however, lacks the ability to convert a string to an integer using an arbitrary radix—only decimal, octal, and hexadecimal formats are supported.

Table 14. Alphabetical List of ANSI C Data Conversion Routines

Name of Routine	Description
atof	Converts a string to a double precision floating point value.
atoi	Converts a string to an integer.
atol	Converts a string to a long integer.
strtod	Converts a string to a double precision floating point value.
strtol	Converts a string to a long integer.
strtoul	Converts a string to an unsigned long integer.

Table 15. ANSI C Data Conversion Routines by Task

Task	Name of Routines
Convert character string to floating point value	atof, strtod
Convert character string to integer	atoi
Convert character string to long integer	atol, strtol
Convert character string to unsigned long integer	strtoul

ANSI C MATH ROUTINES

In addition to the support for basic floating-point operations in the language, the ANSI C library also includes a set of functions—the math functions—to compute common mathematical functions such as the sine and the cosine. Table 16 lists the math routines alphabetically, and Table 17 groups them by task.

Table 16. Alphabetical List of ANSI Math Routines

Name of Routine	Description
abs	Returns the absolute value of an integer argument.
acos	Computes the arc cosine of a value between -1 and 1 and returns an angle between 0 and pi radian.
asin	Computes the arc sine of a value between -1 and 1 and returns an angle between -pi/2 and pi/2 radians.
atan	Computes the arc tangent of a value and returns an angle between -pi/2 and pi/2 radians.
atan2	Computes the arc tangent of one argument divided by the other and returns an angle between -pi and pi radians.
ceil	Finds the smallest integer larger than or equal to the function's floating-point argument.
cos	Evaluates the cosine of an angle in radians.
cosh	Evaluates the hyperbolic cosine of its argument.
div	Divides one integer by another and returns an integer quotient and an integer remainder.
exp	Computes the exponential of a floating-point argument.
fabs	Returns the absolute value of a floating-point argument.
floor	Finds the largest integer smaller than or equal to the function's floating-point argument.
fmod	Computes the floating-point remainder after dividing one floating-point value by another so that the quotient is the largest possible integer for that division.
frexp	Breaks down a floating-point value into a mantissa between 0.5 and 1 and an integer exponent so that the value is equal to the mantissa times two raised to the power of the exponent.
labs	Returns the absolute value of a long integer argument.
ldexp	Computes a floating-point value equal to a mantissa times two raised to the power of an integer exponent.
ldiv	Divides one long integer by another and returns a long integer quotient and a long integer remainder.
log	Evaluates the natural logarithm of its floating-point argument.
log10	Evaluates the logarithm to the base 10 of its floating-point argument.
modf	Breaks down a floating-point value into its integer part and its fractional part.
pow	Computes the value of one argument raised to the power of a second one.
rand	Returns a random integer between 0 and RAND_MAX (defined in stdlib.h).

(continued)

Table 16 *(continued)*

Name of Routine	Description
sin	Evaluates the sine of an angle in radians.
sinh	Evaluates the hyperbolic sine of its argument.
sqrt	Computes the square root of a positive floating point number.
srand	Sets the starting point for the sequence of random numbers generated by rand.
tan	Evaluates the tangent of an angle in radians.
tanh	Evaluates the hyperbolic tangent of its argument.

Table 17. ANSI Math Routines by Task

Task	Name of Routines
Evaluate trigonometric functions	acos, asin, atan, atan2, cos, sin, tan
Evaluate powers and logarithms	exp, frexp, ldexp, log, log10, pow
Compute square root	sqrt
Compute magnitudes and absolute values	abs, fabs
Find integer limits (lower and upper) for floating-point numbers	ceil, floor
Evaluate hyperbolic functions	cosh, sinh, tanh
Break down floating-point number into integer and fraction	modf
Find floating-point remainder	fmod
Integer arithmetic	abs, div, labs, ldiv
Generate random numbers	rand, srand

ANSI CHARACTER CLASSIFICATION AND CONVERSION ROUTINES

Character classification routines (actually macros) beginning with "is" classify a character by various criteria such as whether it is part of the alphabet, a number, a punctuation mark, and so on. The routines *tolower* and *toupper* convert characters to lower and upper case respectively.

Table 18 lists the character classification and conversion routines alphabetically, and Table 19 groups them by task.

Table 18. Alphabetical List of ANSI C Character Classification and Conversion Routines

Name of Function	Description
isalnum	Tests if a character is alphanumeric.
isalpha	Tests if a character is alphabetic.
iscntrl	Tests if a character belongs to the set of control characters.
isdigit	Tests if a character is a numerical digit.
isgraph	Tests if a character is printable (excluding the space character).
islower	Tests if a character is lowercase.
isprint	Tests if a character is printable (includes space).
ispunct	Tests if a character belongs to the set of punctuation characters.
isspace	Tests if a character belongs to the set of "whitespace" characters.
isupper	Tests if a character is uppercase.
isxdigit	Tests if a character is a hexadecimal digit.
tolower	Converts a character to lowercase only if that character is an uppercase letter.
toupper	Converts a character to uppercase only if that character is a lowercase letter.

Table 19. ANSI Character Classification and Conversion Routines by Task

Task	Name of Functions
Classify a character	isalnum, isalpha, iscntrl, isdigit, isgraph, islower, isprint, ispunct, isspace, isupper, isxdigit
Convert from uppercase to lowercase	tolower
Convert from lowercase to uppercase	toupper

ANSI STRING AND BUFFER MANIPULATION ROUTINES

Manipulating text is a major part of many computer applications. The manipulation might involve text editing, word processing, or that part of your application which reads commands typed by the user and interprets them. Typically you read a single line of command into a C string and intrepret it. Depending on the syntax of your application's command set, the interpretation will involve chores such as extracting the commands and parameters from the string, comparing the command against entries in a stored table, or copying the parameters into separate strings for later use. Although C has no built-in operators for handling strings, the ANSI C standard specifies a set of string manipulation routines that provides all the capabilities needed to process strings. Note that "multibyte characters" are new and are not supported by all otherwise ANSI-compliant compilers. They are useful mainly for dealing with special character sets and international alphabets.

Table 20 lists the string and buffer routines alphabetically, and Table 21 groups them by task.

Table 20. Alphabetical List of ANSI String and Buffer Manipulation Routines

Name of Routine	Description
mblen	Returns the number of bytes that makes up a single multibyte character.
mbtowc	Converts a multibyte character to wchar_t type.
mbstowcs	Converts a sequence of multibyte characters into a sequence of codes of wchar_t type.
memchr	Searches for a specific character in a given number of bytes of the buffer.
memcmp	Compares a specified number of bytes of two buffers.
memcpy	Copies a specified number of bytes from one buffer to another (*not for overlapping source and destination*).
memmove	Copies a specified number of bytes from one buffer to another (*handles overlapping source and destination*).
memset	Sets specified number of bytes of a buffer to a given value.
strcat	Appends one string to another.
strchr	Locates the first occurrence of a character in a string.
strcmp	Compares one string to another and differentiates between lowercase and uppercase letters.
strcoll	Compares two strings using a collating sequence specified by the LC_COLLATE category of current locale.
strcpy	Copies one string to another.
strcspn	Returns the position in the string, of the first character that belongs to a given set of characters.
strerror	Returns a string containing the system error message corresponding to an error number.

(continued)

Table 20 *(continued)*

Name of Routine	Description
strlen	Returns the length of a string as the number of bytes in the string excluding the terminating null ('\0').
strncat	Appends a specifed number of characters of one string to another.
strncmp	Compares a specified number of characters of two strings while maintaining the distinction between lowercase and uppercase letters.
strncpy	Copies a specified number of characters from one string to another (Note: resulting string will not automatically have a null character '\0' appended.)
strpbrk	Locates the first occurrence of any character from one string in another.
strrchr	Locates the last occurrence of a character in a string.
strspn	Returns the position in the string of the first character that does not belong to a given set of characters.
strstr	Locates the first occurrence of one string in another.
strtok	Returns the next token in a string with the token delimiters specified in a string.
strxfrm	Transforms a string to a new form so that if strcmp is applied to two transformed strings the returned result is the same as that returned when strcoll is applied to the original strings.
wctomb	Converts a character of wchar_t type to a multibyte character.
wcstombs	Converts a sequence of codes of wchar_t type sequence of multibyte characters.

Table 21. ANSI String and Buffer Manipulation Routines by Task

Task	Name of Routines
Find length of a string	mblen, strlen
Compare two strings or buffers	memcmp, strcmp, strncmp, strcoll, strxfrm
Copy and append	memcpy, memmove, strcat, strcpy, strncat, strncpy
Search for a character or a substring	memchr, strchr, strcspn, strpbrk, strrchr, strspn, strstr
Extract tokens from a string	strtok
Load the same character into every position in a buffer	memset
Prepare error message in a string	strerror
Convert between multibyte and wide character types	mbtowc, mbstowcs, wctomb, wcstombs

ANSI SEARCHING AND SORTING ROUTINES

Searching and sorting are commonplace in many applications. All commercial data base programs have these capabilities. If you implement your own data base program tailored to your specific requirements, you will invariably need search and sort capabilities. For example, if your data base contains the names and addresses of the customers of your company, you will often need to search the list for the information about a certain customer. And for mailings, you might want to print labels for all entries in your data base, sorted by the ZIP code.

If you are developing your data base in C, the ANSI C standard makes your job easier by providing two library routines for sorting and searching lists in memory, as described in Table 22. (See the main alphabetical reference for more details.)

Table 22. Alphabetical List of Searching and Sorting Routines

Name of Routine	Description
bsearch	Search for an element in a sorted array.
qsort	Sort an array of elements.

ANSI TIME AND DATE ROUTINES

The ANSI C library includes a set of routines for obtaining and displaying date and time information. These routines are declared in the header file *time.h*. The *time* function is at the heart of these routines. It returns the current date and time in an implementation-defined encoded form.

There are library routines to convert this time into a printable string, and otherwise manipulate it. A list of the time functions classified by task appears in Table 23 while Table 24 shows a complete catalog of the date and time functions.

Table 23. Alphabetical List of ANSI Time Routines

Name of Routine	Description
asctime	Converts time from a structure of type *tm* to a string.
clock	Returns the elapsed processor time in number of ticks.
ctime	Converts time from a value of type *time_t* to a string.
difftime	Computes the difference of two values of type *time_t*.
gmtime	Converts time from a value of type *time_t* to a structure of type *tm* which will correspond to the Greenwich Mean Time.
localtime	Converts time from a value of type *time_t* to a structure of type *tm* which will correspond to the local time.
mktime	Converts the local time from a structure of type *tm* into a value of type *time_t*.
strftime	Prepares a string with date and time values from a *tm* structure, formatted according to a specified format.
time	Returns the current date and time encoded as a value of type *time_t*. The encoding is implementation-dependent.

Table 24. ANSI Time Routines by Task

Task	Name of Routines
Get current date and time	time
Convert time from one form to another	asctime, ctime, gmtime, localtime, mktime
Compute elapsed time	clock, difftime

USING THE ALPHABETICAL REFERENCE

As noted earlier, the main reference lists everything—functions, macros, data types, keywords, and so on—in a single sequence. You should find this reference to be easy to use, but the following notes will help you get started.

Alphabetization

The alphabetization follows these rules:

- Items that have only non-alphabetic characters, such as most of the operators, are placed together in one sequence in ASCII character order before the first "a" entry.

- Non-alphabetic characters such as /, #, or _ at the beginning of alphabetic items are disregarded. Thus *#define* is treated as though it were *define.*
- Items with underscores inside them are treated as though the underscores spaced the name into separate words. Thus *L_tmpnam* is filed as *L tmpnam* and comes before *LC_ALL* since *LC* comes after *L.*
- Case is always disregarded.

Format of Entries

Each entry contains at least some of the following elements—not all entries have all of them.

Purpose
Briefly describes the purpose for which the item is used and the essential details of its behavior.

Syntax
Describes the format needed to use the item—for example the arguments and data types used when calling a function.

Example Use
An actual statement or expression using the item.

Returns
The value or values that can be returned by the item

See Also
Related items—either other items that do similar things or other items that do different things with the same type of data or variable.

! Logical NOT operator

Purpose

Use the logical *NOT* operator to change a condition to its opposite truth value. *NOT* makes a true condition false and a false condition true.

Syntax

```
!<condition>
```

Example Use

```
!x      /* 1 (true) if x is 0, else 0 (false) */
```

See Also

```
&&, ||
```

!= Not equal operator

Purpose

Use the *not equal* operator to test whether two numeric quantities are not equal to each other, or two strings are not the same.

Syntax

```
expression1 != expression2
```

Example Use

```
x!=y /* 1 (true) if x and y are unequal, else 0
        (false) */
```

See Also

```
==, <, >
```

String-izing preprocessor operator

Purpose

Use the *string-izing* operator to have the preprocessor make a string out of the item that immediately follows the operator. It does this by putting the value in quotes.

Syntax

```
#item
```

Example Use

```
#define value_now(x) printf(#x" = %d\n", x)
value_now(counter);
/* the preprocessor generates this statement:
   printf("counter"" = %d\n", counter);
   which is equivalent to:
   printf("counter = %d\n", counter); */
```

See Also

```
## (token-pasting operator), #define
```

Token-pasting preprocessor operator

Purpose

Use the *token-pasting operator* to join one separate item (token) to another one to form a new token.

Syntax

```
<token1>##<token2>
```

Example Use

```
#define version(x) MSC##x
/* version(6) results in the token MSC6 */
```

See Also

```
# (string-izing operator), #define
```

% Modulus operator

Purpose

Use the *modulus operator* to obtain the remainder after one quantity is divided by another.

Syntax

```
val1 % val2
```

Example Use

```
Remainder = 18 % 7 /* assigns 4 to Remainder */
```

See Also

```
/, div, 1div, mod, modf
```

& Address-of operator

Purpose

Use the *address-of* operator to get the address at which the value of variable is stored.

Syntax

```
&<varname>
```

Example Use

```
Addr = &x  /* assign address of x to Addr */
```

See Also

```
* (pointer dereferencing operator), sizeof
```

&
Bitwise AND operator

Purpose

Use the *bitwise AND operator* to compare two quantities bit by bit. Each bit in the resulting value will be set to 1 if and only if the corresponding bits in the values being compared were both set to 1. Do not confuse & (bitwise AND) with && (logical AND); the latter compares the whole values, not individual bits.

Syntax

```
val1 & val2
```

Example Use

```
Result = 11 AND 8; /* 1011 AND 1000 results in 1000 */
```

See Also

```
|, ~, &&, ||
```

&&
Logical AND operator

Purpose

Use the *logical AND operator* to check whether two conditions are both true. The *AND* operator returns a value of 1 (true) only if both of the conditions tested are true (1). Do not confuse && (logical and) with & (bitwise AND); the latter compares individual bits and sets the bits in the result accordingly.

Syntax

```
val1 && val2
```

Example Use

```
if (Category == CLERICAL && Years_Served >= 10)
/* True only if clerical category and at least 10
   years is true have been served */
```

See Also

```
||, !
```

()
Function argument list operator

Purpose

Use parentheses to enclose arguments in function calls and parameter lists in function declarations. An argument is an actual value sent to a function, while a parameter is a formal description of the argument in the function declaration.

Syntax

```
func_name(type parameter_name, ...) /* function
                                       declaration */
func_name(argument, ...)            /* function call */
```

Example Use

```
void *malloc(size_t num_bytes);
                       /* declaration of malloc
                          specifies an argument size_t
                          num_bytes */
malloc(10)             /* call malloc with argument
                          10 */
```

*
Pointer dereferencing operator

Purpose

Use the *pointer dereferencing operator* to get the value stored at the address represented by a pointer.

Syntax

```
*pointer_name      /* value pointed to by pointer */
```

Example Use

```
Val = *p;      /* assigns contents of location whose
                  address is stored in pointer p */
```

See Also

&, =>, []

*
Multiplication operator

Purpose

Use the *multiplication operator* to multiply two values.

Syntax

```
val1 * val2
```

Example Use

```
Product = x * y   /* assigns product of x and y to
                     Product */
```

See Also

+, -, /, %

+ Addition operator

Purpose

Use the *addition operator* to add two values together.

Syntax

```
val1 + val2
```

Example Use

```
Total = Price + Tax;    /* Adds Price and Tax and
                           assigns to Total */
```

See Also

-, *, /, %

+ Unary Plus operator

Purpose

Use the *unary plus operator* to make a value positive.

Syntax

```
+val
```

Example Use

```
+x     /* Value of x is positive (new in ANSI C) */
```

See Also

- (unary minus operator)

++ Increment operator

Purpose

Use the *increment operator* to add one to the value of a variable. This is often done to increase loop index variables by one each time through the loop. The ultimate effect of *i++* is the same as that of *i = i + 1;*.

When the *increment operator* precedes the variable name (for example, *++i*) the value of *i* is increased by one before any expression containing *i* is evaluated. When the *increment operator* follows the variable name (for example, *i++*) the value of *i* is increased by one *after* the expression containing *i* is evaluated.

Syntax

```
++val        /* pre-increment */
val++        /* post-increment */
```

Example Use

```
for (i=0, sum=0; i <= limit; sum += i, i++)
/* i is incremented only after it is added to the
   sum */
++counter    /* counter is incremented before it is
                used for anything*/
i++, j++     /* first increment i, then increment j */
```

See Also

`+, +=`

,
Sequential evaluation operator

Purpose

Use the *sequential evaluation operator* (a comma) to group together two or more expressions that will be evaluated in succession from left to right. This operator is often used in *for* loops to perform two or more initializations or updates.

Syntax

```
<expression>, <expression> ...
```

Example Use

```
ii++, j++    /* first increment i, then increment j */
```

See Also

`for`

-
Negation operator

Purpose

Use the *negation operator* to make a quantitiy negative. (This operator is sometimes called the unary minus operator).

Syntax

```
-val
```

Example Use

```
x = 10
y = -x      /* y = -10 */
```

See Also

`+ (unary plus operator), - (subtraction operator)`

-
Subtraction operator

Purpose

Use the *subtraction operator* to subtract one value from another.

Syntax

```
val1 - val2
```

Example Use

```
Diff = X1 - X2    /* subtract X2 from X1 and assign to
                     Diff */
```

See Also

```
- (negation operator)
```

--
Decrement operator

Purpose

Use the *decrement operator* to subtract *one* from the value of a variable. This is often done to decrease loop index variables by one each time through the loop. The ultimate effect of *i* -- is the same as that of *i* = *i* -*1;*.

When the *decrement operator* precedes the variable name (for example, --*i*) the value of *i* is decreased by one before any expression containing *i* is evaluated. When the *decrement operator* follows the variable name (for example, *i*--) the value of *i* is decreased by one *after* the expression containing *i* is evaluated.

Syntax

```
--val        /* pre-decrement */
val--        /* post-decrement */
```

Example Use

```
for (i=MAX_VAL, sum=0; i >= MIN_VAL; sum += i, i--)
/* i is decremented only after it is added to the sum */
--counter    /* counter is decremented before it is
                used for anything */
i--, j--     /* first decrement i, then decrement j */
```

See Also

```
-, -=
```

->
Pointer member selection operator

Purpose

Use the *pointer member selection operator* to access a particular field in a structure pointed to by a pointer. The notation *struc_pointer -> member* returns the *member* field of the *struc* pointed to by *struc_pointer.* If you want to access a member of a structure directly (not through a pointer) use the notation *struc_var_name.member_name* where *struc_var_name* is a variable of a *struc* type and *member_name* is the name of the member (field).

Syntax

```
struc_ptr->member_name
```

Example Use

```
struct corp_info
{                          /*define a structure */
   char * name
   ...
};
struct corp_info corp;     /* define a variable of
                              that type */
struct corp_info *ptr = corp;   /* define pointer to
                                   the structure */
ptr->name = "Microsoft"; /* assign value to member
                            through pointer */
```

See Also

```
.(member selection operator), struct
```

.
Member selection operator

Purpose

Use the *member selection operator* to access a member (field) of a pointer directly. The notation *struc_var_name.member_name* accesses member *member_name* of *struct* variable *struc_var_name.* To access a structure through a pointer, use the *pointer member selection operator* (->) instead.

Syntax

```
struc_name.member_name
```

Example Use

```
struct address             /* define a structure */
{
```

```
    char * name
    ...
};
struct address this_address;    /* define a variable
                                    of that type */
this_address.name = "John Q. Public"  /* assign value
                                          to member of
                                          structure */
```

See Also

`->, struct`

/ Division operator

Purpose

Use the *division operator* to divide one numeric value by another. For integer values the whole-number quotient is returned; for floating-point type values the decimal fraction is returned.

Syntax

```
val1 / val2
```

Example Use

```
quotient = dividend / divisor;  /* Divide dividend by
                                    divisor */
```

See Also

`+, -, *, %`

< Less-than operator

Purpose

Use the *less-than operator* to determine whether a numeric value is less than another numeric value, or whether a character or string comes before another character or string in the collating sequence.

The *less-than operator* returns 1 (true) if the first value is less than (or comes before) the second one; otherwise the operator returns 0 (false).

Syntax

```
val1 < val2
```

Example Use

```
if (score > goal) printf("You won!\n");
```

See Also

`>, =, !=`

<<
Left shift operator

Purpose

Use the *left shift operator* to shift all of the bits in a value to the left. Each time you shift the leftmost bit is discarded. A shift of one bit to the left is equivalent to multiplying the value by 2.

Syntax

```
value << <number of times to shift>
```

Example Use

```
x = 2
x = x << 4;          /* x shifted to the left by 4 bit
                        positions and now equals 64 */
```

See Also

```
>>, &, |
```

<=
Less than or equal to operator

Purpose

Use the *less than or equal to* operator to determine whether one numeric value is either less than or equal to another. If the second value is less than or equal, the operator returns 1 (true). If the second value is greater than the first, the operator returns 0 (false).

Syntax

```
val1 <= val2
```

Example Use

```
if temperature <= critical_point printf("Everything's
fine!\n");
```

See Also

```
==, >, >=
```

=
Assignment operator

Purpose

Use the *assignment operator* to assign a value to a variable. Do not confuse = with ==, the latter operator does not assign a value but rather tests the value for equality.

Syntax

```
varname =  value;  /* assign value to variable */
var1 = var2 = value;      /* assign same value to two
                             or more variables */
```

You can combine an arithmetic operator (+, -, *, or /) with the assignment operator. When you do so the indicated arithmetic is performed using the variable and the second value, and the result is assigned to the variable. For example:

```
a += b        /* add b to a and assign result to a */
a *= 2        /* multiply a times 2 and make that the
                 new value of a */
```

Example Use

```
total = 0;            /* assign 0 to total */
line = word = 1;      /* assign 1 to both line and word */
counter += value; /* increase counter by value */
```

See Also

`=, ++, --`

==
Equal to operator

Purpose

Use the *equal to* operator to determine whether the first value is equal to the second one. For numbers this means that both have the same value; for characters or strings equality means that both characters or strings are the same. The operator returns 1 (true) if the values are equal; otherwise it returns false (0).

Do not confuse == with = ; the latter does not compare the second value to the first, but rather assigns the second value to the first.

Syntax

```
val1 == val2
```

Example Use

```
if (cust_no == target_no) flag_account(cust_no);
if (choice == 'a') do_choice_a;
```

See Also

`<=, >=, !=`

>
Greater than operator

Purpose

Use the *greater than operator* to determine whether the first value is greater than the second one. For numbers this means that the first number is larger than the second; for characters or strings it means that the first character or string comes later than the second one in the collating sequence. The operator returns the value 1 (true) if the first value is greater than (or comes later than) the second; otherwise the operator returns 0 (false).

Syntax

```
val1 > val2
```

Example Use

```
if (line > lines_per page) do_header();
if (choice > 'f') menu_error();
```

See Also

```
<, <=, ==, !=
```

>> Right shift operator

Purpose

Use the *right shift operator* to shift all of the bits in a value to the right. Each time you shift the rightmost bit is discarded. A shift of one bit to the right is equivalent to dividing the value by 2.

Syntax

```
value >> <number of times to shift>
```

Example Use

```
x = 16
x = x >> 1;  /* x shifted to the right by 1 bit
                position and now equals 8 */
```

See Also

```
<<, &, |
```

[] Array element reference operator

Purpose

Use the *array element reference operator* to access the indicated element of an array using a numeric subscript. Note that arrays in C begin with element number 0; for an element declared to have *n* elements the highest legal subscript is *n - 1.*

Syntax

```
array_name[element_number]
```

Example Use

```
int total [10];   /* declare array of integer */
total[1] = 25;    /* assign 25 to element 1 of array */
```

```
totalC0] = subtotal;  /* assign value of subtotal to
                         first (0) element of the ar
                         ray */
```

^ Bitwise exclusive OR operator

Purpose

Use the *bitwise exclusive OR operator* to compare two values bit by bit such that the resulting value has a 1 only in positions where the compared bit values differ. Note that with the *bitwise exclusive OR operator* the result has a 0 in any position where the compared values are either both 1 or both 0. The *bitwise or operator*, on the other hand, has a 1 in the resulting position where at least one of the compared bits is a 1.

Syntax

```
val1 ^ val2
```

Example Use

```
bitvals = 6 ^ 10;  /* 0110 ^ 1010; bitvals has value
                      1100 */
```

See Also

|, &, ~

| Bitwise OR operator

Purpose

Use the *bitwise OR operator* to compare two values bit by bit such that the resulting value has a 1 in positions where one or both of the compared values have a 1. This differs from the *bitwise exclusive OR operator* in that latter puts a 1 in the resulting position if one and only one of the compared values has a 1 in that position.

Syntax

```
val1 | val2
```

Example Use

```
bitvals = 6 | 10;  /* 0110 | 1010; bitvals has value
                      1110 */
```

See Also

^, &, ~

||
Logical OR operator

Purpose

Use the *logical OR operator* to determine whether at least one of two conditions is true. The operator returns 1 (true) if one or both of the conditions is true, but returns 0 (false) if both are false.

Syntax

```
condition1 || condition2
```

Example Use

```
if ((temperature > BOILING_POINT) || (pressure >
BURSTING_POINT)) sound_alarm()
```

See Also

```
&&, !
```

~
Bitwise negation operator

Purpose

Use the *bitwise negation operator* to reverse each bit position in a value such that ones become zeros and zeros become ones.

Example Use

```
bitvals =  40;            /* 00101000 */
newvals = ~bitvals        /* 11010111 */
```

See Also

```
&, !
```

? :
Conditional operator

Purpose

Use the *conditional operator* to choose one of two expressions based on the truth of a condition.

Syntax

```
condition ? expression1 : expression2
```

If the condition is true (1) then expression1 is evaluated, otherwise expression2 is evaluated. The expressions are often alternative assignments as shown below. This conditional statement is equivalent to

```
if (condition)
      expression1;
else
      expression2;
```

Example Use

```
a > b ? max = a : max = b;
/* max becomes a if a is greater, otherwise
   max becomes b */
```

See Also

`if statement`

\a escape sequence for "alert"

Purpose

Use the *\a* escape sequence to have a string sound an alert (usually a beep) on the system's speaker. The position of the cursor or print head is not changed.

Example Use

```
printf("Do you really want to reformat this disk?\a");
```

See Also

`printf`

abort

Purpose

Use *abort* to abnormally exit your program. *abort* calls *raise(SIGABRT)*. Note that unlike *exit*, *abort* will not flush the file buffers or call the routines set up by *atexit*. However, you can take care of these chores by appropriately setting up the processing for the SIGABRT signal.

Syntax

```
#include <stdlib.h>
void abort(void);
```

Example Use

```
abort();
```

See Also

`atexit, exit, raise, signal, SIGABRT`

abs

Purpose

Use the *abs* function to get the absolute value of the integer argument *n*.

Syntax

```
#include <stdlib.h>
int abs(int n);
int n;          Interger whose absolute value is returned
```

Example Use

```
x = abs(-5); /* x will be 5 now */
```

Returns

The integer returned by *abs* is the absolute value of n.

See Also

```
fabs, labs
```

acos

Purpose

Use the *acos* function to compute the arccosine of an argument *x* whose value lies in the range -1 to 1. The result is an angle with a value between 0 and pi radians. You can convert an angle from radians to degrees by multiplying it by 57.29578.

Syntax

```
#include <math.h>
double acos(double x);
double x;          Argument whose arccosine is to be computed
```

Example Use

```
angle = acos(0.5); /* angle is pi/3 */
```

Returns

When the value of the argument *x* is in the valid range of -1 to 1, *acos* returns the arccosine. Otherwise, a domain error occurs.

See Also

```
cos
```

argc

Purpose

The value *argc*, supported by many operating systems including UNIX and MS-DOS, is used in the call to *main* that starts the program. *argc* is the number of arguments used on the command line, including the name of the program and any command-line switches, file names, etc. that the user supplied.

Syntax

```
main (int argc, char **argv); /* typical declaration
                                  of main() */
```

Example Use

```
if (argc < 2)

{
   printf("You must supply at least two arguments\n");
   exit (EXIT_FAILURE);    /* return to operating
                              system */
};
```

See Also

argv, getenv

argv

Purpose

The value *argv*, supported by many operating systems including UNIX and MS-DOS, is used in the call to *main* that starts the program. *argv* is a pointer to an array of character strings; each string is one of the arguments that the user typed on the command line. *argv[0]* is usually the name of the program itself, and the successive arguments are the option switches, filenames, and so on that the user typed.

Syntax

```
main (int argc, char **argv); /* typical declaration
                                  of main() */
```

Sample Use

```
/* one way for a program to access its arguments */
for (i = 1; i < argc; i++)
      printf("%s", argv[i]);
```

See Also

argc, getemv

asctime

Purpose

Use the *asctime* function to convert to a character string the value of a time stored in the structure of type *tm* at the address *time.* The structure *tm* is defined in time.h as follows:

```
struct tm
{
  int tm_sec;   /* seconds after the minute - [0,60]*/
  int tm_min;   /* minutes after the hour - [0,59] */
  int tm_hour;  /* hours since midnight - [0,23]   */
  int tm_mday;  /* day of the month - [1,31]       */
  int tm_mon;   /* months since January - [0,11]   */
  int tm_year;  /* years since 1900                */
  int tm_wday;  /* days since Sunday - [0,6]       */
  int tm_yday;  /* days since January 1 - [0,365]  */
  int tm_isdst; /* daylight savings time flag      */
};
```

The string prepared by *asctime* will be 26 characters long, counting the null character ('\0') at the end, and has the form:

```
Thu Jul 21 19:02:39 1990\n\0
```

As the example shows, a 24-hour clock is used for the time.

Syntax

```
#include <time.h>
char *asctime(struct tm *time);
struct tm *time;
```

Pointer to a structure containing time to be converted to a string

Example Use

```
printf("The time is %s\n", asctime(&timedata));
```

Returns

The *asctime* function returns a pointer to the static data area where the string is stored.

See Also

ctime, gmtime, localtime, time, tm

asin

Purpose

Use the *asin* function to compute the arcsine of the argument *x* provided its value lies in the range -1 to 1. The result is an angle with a value between -pi/2 and pi/2 radians. You can convert an angle from radians to degrees by multiplying it by 57.29578.

Syntax

```
#include <math.h>
```

```
double asin(double x);
double x;
```
Argument whose arcsine is to be computed

Example Use

```
angle = asin(0.707)  /* angle is roughly pi/4 */
```

Returns

For a valid argument *x* with values between -1 and 1, *asin* returns an angle whose sine is equal to *x*. However, if the argument's value lies outside the acceptable range, a domain error occurs.

See Also

```
sin
```

assert

Purpose

Use the *assert* macro to print an error message and abort the program if the <expression> is false. The *assert* macro is typically used to identify program errors during the debugging phase. After the program is debugged, you can disable all occurrences of the *assert* macros by defining the preprocessor macro NDEBUG.

Syntax

```
#include <assert.h>
void assert(<expression>);
<expression>
```
C statements specifying assertion being tested

Example Use

```
assert(arg_value >= 0);
```

See Also

```
abort, NDEBUG
```

atan

Purpose

Use the *atan* function to compute the arctangent of the argument *x*. The result will be an angle with value between -pi/2 and pi/2 radians. You can convert an angle from radians to degrees by multiplying it by 57.29578.

Syntax

```
#include <math.h>
```

```
double atan(double x);
double x;                    Argument whose arctangent is to be computed
```

Example Use

```
angle = atan(1.0)  /* angle is "pi"/4  */
```

Returns

The *atan* function returns the angle in the range -pi/2 and pi/2 whose tangent is equal to *x*.

See Also

```
atan2, tan
```

atan2

Purpose

Use the *atan2* function to compute the arctangent of the ratio of the arguments *y/x*. The result will be an angle with value between -pi and pi radians. You can convert an angle from radians to degrees by multiplying it by 57.29578. In contrast to *atan* which takes a single argument, *atan2* takes two arguments and uses the sign of the two arguments to determine the quadrant (90 degree sector in cartesian coordinates) in which the angle should lie.

Syntax

```
#include <math.h>
double atan2(double y, double x);
double x, y;                 Arctangent of y/x will be computed
```

Example Use

```
angle = atan2(y, x);
```

Returns

Provided both arguments *x* and *y* are non-zero, *atan2* returns an angle whose tangent is equal to *x*. However, if both arguments are zero, a domain error may occur.

See Also

```
atan, tan
```

atexit

Purpose

Use *atexit* to set up a stack of up to 32 (this is the minimum number specified by ANSI C) functions that the system will call in a "last-in first-out" manner when your program terminates normally. Note that the functions passed to *atexit* can not take any arguments. This feature is useful for setting up house cleaning chores that may be performed upon program termination.

Syntax

```
#include <stdlib.h>
int atexit(void (*func)(void));
void (*func)(void);                 Pointer to function to be called
```

Example Use

```
atexit(cleanup_all);
```

Returns

The *atexit* function returns a zero if successful. Otherwise, it returns a non-zero value.

See Also

exit

atof

Purpose

Use the *atof* function to convert the argument *string* into a double value. A call to *atof* is equivalent to the call *strtod(string, (char **)NULL)*.

Syntax

```
#include <stdlib.h>
double atof(const char *string);
const char *string;                 String to be converted
```

Example Use

```
dbl_value = atof(input_string);
```

Returns

The *atof* function returns the double precision value after conversion.

See Also

atoi, atol, strtod, NULL

atoi

Purpose

Use the *atoi* function to convert the argument *string* into an *int* value. A call to *atoi* is equivalent to the call *(int)strtol(string, (char **)NULL, 10).*

Syntax

```
#include <stdlib.h>
int atoi(const char *string);
const char *string;                String to be converted
```

Example Use

```
int_value = atoi(input_string);
```

Returns

The *atoi* function returns the integer value as an *int* variable.

See Also

atof, atol, strtol, strtoul, NULL

atol

Purpose

Use the *atol* function to convert the argument *string* into a *long* integer value. A call to *atol* is equivalent to the call *strol (string, (char**) NULL, 10).*

Syntax

```
# include <stdi.b.h>
int atol (const char*string);
const char *string;        String to be converted
```

Example Use

```
long_value = atol(input_string);
```

Returns

The *atol* function returns the converted value as a long variable.

See Also

atof, atoi, strtol, strtoul, NULL

auto

Purpose

Use the *auto* storage class specifier to declare temporary variables. These variables are created upon entering a block statement and destoyed upon exit. Local variables of a function have the *auto* storage class by default.

Syntax

```
auto <type> <varname>
```

Example Use

```
/* the variables i, limit, and sum are created only
   when the if statement is true—when the user
   presses a 'C' */
#include <stdio.h>
main()
{
     int c;
     c = getchar();
     if(c == 'C')
     {
          auto int i, limit, sum;
          printf("Sum from 1 to ?");
          scanf(" %d",&limit);
          /* Compute sum from 1 to limit */
          for(i=0, sum=0; i <= limit; sum += i, i++);
          printf("\nSum from 1 to %d = %d\n", limit,
          sum);
     }
}
```

See Also

extern, register, static

\b escape sequence for backspace

Purpose

Use the *\b* escape sequence to move the cursor or print head back one space. Other effects depend on the hardware in use.

Example Use

```
/* backs up to start of last word printed */
for (pos = 1; pos < len(word); pos++)
       putc("\b");
```

See Also

printf, \r, \n

break

Purpose

Use the *break* keyword to exit the innermost *do, while,* or *for* loop. It is also used to exit from a *switch* statement.

Syntax

```
break;
```

Example Use

```
/* add the numbers from 1 to 10 in an endless loop.
   Use break to exit the loop  */
sum = 0;
i = 0;
while(1)
{
    sum += i;
    i++;
    if(i > 10) break;
}
```

See Also

case, do, for, switch, while

bsearch

Purpose

Use the *bsearch* function to search a sorted array beginning at the address *base* and comprising *num* elements, each of size *width* bytes. The argument *key* points to the value being sought. Note that you can use the *qsort* routine to sort the array before calling *bsearch.*

Syntax

```
#include <stdlib.h>
void *bsearch(const void *key, const void *base,
size_t num, size_t width, int (*compare)(const void
*elem1, const void *elem2));
```

`const void *key;`	*Pointer to element value being searched for*
`const void *base;`	*Pointer to beginning of array being searched*
`size_t     num;`	*Number of elements in array*
`size_t     width;`	*Size of each element in bytes*
`int (*compare)(const void *elem1, const void *elem2);`	*Pointer to a function that compares two elements* elem1 *and* elem2 *each of type* const void *

Example Use

```
int mycompare(const void *, const void *);
result = (char **) bsearch((const void *)keyword,
                           (const void *)envp,
                           (size_t)count,
                           (size_t)sizeof(char *),
                            mycompare);
```

Returns

The *bsearch* function returns a pointer to the first occurrence of the value *key* in the array. If the value is not found, *bsearch* returns a NULL.

See Also

`qsort, NULL, size_t`

BUFSIZ

Purpose

The *BUFSIZ* predefined value gives the size of the buffer used by *setbuf*. It is defined in LIMITS.H.

See Also

`FOPEN_MAX`

calloc

Purpose

Use *calloc* to allocate memory for an array of *num_elems* elements each of size *elem_size* bytes. All bytes of the allocated array will be initialized to zero.

Syntax

```
#include <stdlib.h>
void *calloc(size_t num_elems, size_t elem_size);
size_t   num_elems;          Number of elements
size_t   elem_size;          Size of each element in bytes
```

Example Use

```
p_int = (int *) calloc(100, sizeof(int));
```

Returns

The return value from *calloc* is a pointer to *void*, representing the address of the allocated memory. If the memory allocation is unsuccessful because of insufficient space or bad values of the arguments, a NULL is returned.

See Also

```
free, malloc, realloc, NULL, size_t
```

case

Purpose

Use the *case* keyword to label cases in a *switch* statement. If the switch variable has the specified value the statements associated with the case are executed. A *break* statement is used at the end of the statements for each case in order to prevent the next case from being executed, unless that behavior is intended.

Syntax

```
case <value> : <statement; ... >
```

Example Use

```
case 'A': do_choice_A();
          break;
```

See Also

```
default, switch
```

ceil

Purpose

Use the *ceil* function to find the "ceiling" of a *double* argument *x*. The "ceiling" is the smallest integral value that is equal to or that just exceeds *x*. This can be used in rounding a *double* value *up* to the next integer.

Syntax

```
#include <math.h>
double ceil(double x);
double x;             Variable whose "ceiling" is to be returned
```

Example Use

```
x_ceiling = ceil(4.1);  /* x_ceiling is 5.0 */
```

Returns

The return value is the "ceiling" of *x* expressed as a *double*.

See Also

```
floor
```

char

Purpose

Use the *char* type specifier to declare character variables and arrays. A character variable actually stores the character's code number in the machine's character set. A *signed char* has a range between -128 and 127, while a regular *char* (occasionally called *unsigned char*) has a range of 0 through 255.

Syntax

```
char <varname>;
```

Example Use

```
/* declare a character, a pointer to a char, and an
   array of characters */
   char c, *p_c, string[80];
```

See Also

`double, float, int, long, short, signed, unsigned`

CHAR_BIT

Purpose

The *CHAR_BIT* predefined value gives the maximum number of bits in *char*. It is defined in LIMITS.H.

See Also

`CHAR_MAX, CHAR_MIN`

CHAR_MAX

Purpose

The *CHAR_MAX* predefined value gives the maximum value of a *char*. It is defined in LIMITS.H.

See Also

`CHAR_MIN, CHAR_BIT`

CHAR_MIN

Purpose

The *CHAR_MIN* predefined value gives the minimum value of a *char*. It is defined in LIMITS.H

See Also

`CHAR_MAX, CHAR_BIT`

clearerr

Purpose
Use *clearerr* to reset the error and end-of-file indicators of the stream specified by the stream pointer *stream.*

Syntax
```
#include <stdio.h>
void clearerr(FILE *stream);
FILE *stream;      Pointer to stream whose error flag is being cleared
```

Example Use
```
clearerr(outfile);
```

See Also
```
ferror, feof, FILE
```

CLK_TCK

Purpose
The *CLK_TCK* predefined value gives the number of clock ticks per second returned by the *clock* function. It is defined in TIME.H.

See Also
```
clock
```

clock

Purpose
Use *clock* to obtain the amount of processor time used by the current process in "number of ticks." The constant CLK_TCK, defined in *time.h* is the number of ticks per second, so the value returned by *clock* should be divided by CLK_TCK to get the elapsed processor time in seconds.

Syntax
```
#include <time.h>
clock_t clock(void);
```

Example Use
```
ticks_now = clock();
```

Returns
If the processor time is available to *clock*, it returns the current time in ticks, cast as a value of type *clock_t* which is defined in *time.h*. Otherwise, it returns the value -1, cast as *clock_t.*

See Also
```
difftime, time, CLK_TCK, clock_t
```

clock_t

Purpose

The *clock_t* data type is capable of holding the value of the time returned by the *clock* function. It is defined in TIME.H.

See Also

`time t, tm`

const

Purpose

Use the *const* type qualifier to indicate that the variable that follows may not be modified by the program. (You can, however, initialize the constant at the time of declaration, as shown in the following examples). You can not later assign a value to a *const*, increment it, or decrement it. Declaring constants can protect key values from change, accommodate data in read-only memory, or improve optimization in some compilers by assuring the compiler that a value will not be changed later. *const* guarantees only that you the programmer will not change the value later; the value may in some cases be changed by the operation of the hardware. You can declare such a hardware-dependent value to be *const volatile.*

Use of *const* is preferable to using *#define* with a numeric literal, because the compiler doesn't provide type-checking in the latter case.

Example Use

```
const short x = 32;      /* x is constant */
const int *p_i = 2048; /* value pointed to by p_i is
                          constant */
int *const p_c_i = ;   /* pointer p_c_i is constant */
```

See Also

`volatile, #define`

continue

Purpose

Use the *continue* keyword to skip execution of the body of a loop. It is equivalent to executing a *goto* to the end of the loop. After skipping the rest of the body of the loop, control returns to the loop condition, which is checked as usual. The *continue* statement affects the innermost loop in which it appears.

Syntax

```
continue;
```

Example Use

```
/* The statement "sum += i;" will be skipped when i
   is 5,giving the sum of the numbers from 1 to 10,
   excluding 5 */
for(i=0, sum=0; i <= 10, i++)
{
    if(i == 5) continue;
    sum += i;
}
```

See Also

for, if, while

cos

Purpose

Use the *cos* function to compute the cosine of *double* argument *x*, which must be expressed in radians. You can convert an angle from degrees to radians by dividing it by 57.29578.

Syntax

```
#include <math.h>
double cos(double x);
double x;              Angle in radians whose cosine is to be computed
```

Example Use

```
cos_angle = cos(ang_radian);
```

Returns

The *cos* function returns the cosine of *x*. If the value of *x* is large in magnitude, the result may be very imprecise.

See Also

acos, sin

cosh

Purpose

Use *cosh* to compute the hyperbolic cosine of *x*.

Syntax

```
#include <math.h>
double cosh(double x);
double x;            Variable whose hyperbolic cosine is to be computed
```

Example Use

```
result = cosh(x);
```

Returns

Normally, *cosh* returns the hyperbolic cosine of *x*. If the value of the result is too large (a *double* variable can be as large as 10^{308}), a range error will occur.

See Also

```
sinh
```

ctime

Purpose

Use the *ctime* function to convert to a character string the value of time stored in the variable of type *time_t* at the address *timer*. Calling *ctime* is equivalent to the call *asctime(localtime(timer))*.

Syntax

```
#include <time.h>
char *ctime(const time_t *timer);
const time_t  *timer;         Pointer to calendar time
```

Example Use

```
printf("Current time = %s\n", ctime(&bintime));
```

Returns

The *ctime* function returns the pointer to the string.

See Also

```
asctime, time, time_t
```

__DATE__ predefined macro

Purpose

Use the *__DATE__* predefined macro to display the date of translation of the source file by the preprocessor. This macro inserts a string constant into the file of the form "MMM DD YYYY" (such as "June 15 1990")

Example Use

```
printf("Compiled on: ");
printf(__DATE__);
```

See Also

`__FILE__, __TIME__, __LINE__, __STDC__`

DBL_DIG

Purpose

The *DBL_DIG* predefined value gives the number of significant decimal digits in a *double* value. It is defined in FLOAT.H.

See Also

`DBL_EPSILON, DBL_MANT_DIG, DBL_MIN, DBL_MIN_10_EXP, DBL_MIN_EXP, DBL_MAX, DBL_MAX_10_EXP, DBL_MAX_EXP`

DBL_EPSILON

Purpose

The *DBL_EPSILON* predefined value gives the smallest positive *double* value *x* such that *1+x != 1.* It is defined in FLOAT.H.

See Also

`DBL_DIG, DBL_MANT_DIG, DBL_MIN, DBL_MIN_10_EXP, DBL_MIN_EXP, DBL_MAX, DBL_MAX_10_EXP, DBL_MAX_EXP`

DBL_MANT_DIG

Purpose

The *DBL_MANT_DIG* predefined value gives the number of base *FLT_RADIX* digits in the mantissa of a *double*. It is defined in FLOAT.H.

See Also

`DBL_DIG, DBL_EPSILON, DBL_MIN, DBL_MIN_10_EXP, DBL_MIN_EXP, DBL_MAX, DBL_MAX_10_EXP, DBL_MAX_EXP`

DBL_MAX

Purpose

The *DBL_MAX* predefined value gives the maximum representable finite value that can be stored in a *double*. It is defined in FLOAT.H.

See Also

`DBL_DIG, DBL_MANT_DIG, DBL_EPSILON, DBL_MIN, DBL_MIN_10_EXP, DBL_MIN_EXP DBL_MAX_10_EXP, DBL_MAX_EXP`

DBL_MAX_10_EXP

Purpose

The *DBL_MAX_10_EXP* predefined value gives the maximum integer such that 10 raised to that power is representable in a *double.*

See Also

`DBL_DIG, DBL_MANT_DIG, DBL_EPSILON, DBL_MIN, DBL_MIN_10_EXP, DBL_MIN_EXP, DBL_MAX, DBL_MAX_EXP`

DBL_MAX_EXP

Purpose

The *DBL_MAX_EXP* predefined value gives the maximum integer such that FLT_RADIX raised to that power is representable in a *double.* It is defined in FLOAT.H.

See Also

`DBL_DIG, DBL_MANT_DIG, DBL_EPSILON, DBL_MIN, DBL_MIN_10_EXP, DBL_MIN_EXP, DBL_MAX, DBL_MAX_10_EXP`

DBL_MIN

Purpose

The *DBL_MIN* predefined value gives the minimum positive floating-point number that can be stored in a *double.* It is defined in FLOAT.H.

See Also

`DBL_DIG, DBL_MANT_DIG, DBL_EPSILON, DBL_MIN_10_EXP, DBL_MIN_EXP, DBL_MAX, DBL_MAX_10_EXP, DBL_MAX_EXP`

DBL_MIN_10_EXP

Purpose

The *DBL_MIN_10_EXP* predefined value gives the minimum negative integer such that 10 raised to that power is representable in a *double.* It is defined in FLOAT.H.

See Also

`DBL_DIG, DBL_MANT_DIG, DBL_EPSILON, DBL_MIN, DBL_MIN_EXP, DBL_MAX, DBL_MAX_10_EXP, DBL_MAX_EXP`

DBL_MIN_EXP

Purpose

The *DBL_MIN_EXP* predefined value gives the minimum negative integer such that FLT_RADIX raised to that power minus 1 is representable in a *double.*

See Also

DBL_DIG, DBL_MANT_DIG, DBL_EPSILON, DBL_MIN, DBL_MIN_10_EXP, DBL_MAX, DBL_MAX_10_EXP, DBL_MAX_EXP

default

Purpose

Use *default* as the label in a *switch* statement to mark code that will be executed when none of the *case* labels match the *switch* expression.

Syntax

```
default: <statement; ..>
```

Example Use

```
default: printf("Unknown command!\n");
```

See Also

case, switch

#define preprocessor definition operator

Purpose

Use the *#define* operator to define a symbol or a macro. A simple definition such as *#define PI 3.14159* simply tells the preprocessor to replace each occurrence of *PI* in the source code with the numeric literal *3.14159*. A macro is a more flexible definition with one or more parameters that control what is actually put into the source code. For example, *#define SQUARE(x) ((x)*(x))* allows you to use a statement such as *SQUARE(2)* your code; the result of this statement is to place *((2)*(2))* or 4 in the code. You can redefine a macro with the same expression as often as you want.

Example Use

```
ZOOM(v, r)  ((v)*(r))
ZOOM(4, 8)  /* puts 4 * 8 or 32 in the code */
```

See Also

(string-izing operator), ## (token-pasting operator)

defined (preprocessor condition)

Purpose

Use the *defined* preprocessor condition to determine whether a preprocessor symbol or macro is defined in the current program. Typically this is used to control conditional compilation.

Syntax

```
defined (symbol)    /* true if symbol is defined */
!defined (symbol)   /* true if symbol is not defined */
```

Note that *#ifdef* is an alternate form of *#if defined* and *#ifndef* is an alternate form of *#if !defined.*

Example Use

```
#if defined (NON_STANDARD)
    #include "ourdefs.h"
#endif
```

difftime

Purpose

Use the *difftime* function to compute the difference between two time values *time2* and *time1*, both of type *time_t.*

Syntax

```
#include <time.h>
double difftime(time_t time2, time_t time1);
time_t time2;        Value of time from which time 1will be subtracted
time_t time1;        Value of time to be subtracted from time2
```

Example Use

```
seconds_used = difftime(oldtime, newtime);
```

Returns

The *difftime* function returns the elapsed time, *time2-time1*, in seconds as a double precision number.

See Also

```
clock, time, time_t
```

div

Purpose

Use the *div* function to divide the first integer *numer* by the second one *denom* and obtain the resulting quotient and remainder packed in a structure of type *div_t.* The structure of type *div_t* is defined in *stdlib.h* as

```
typedef struct
{
    int quot;    /* The quotient  */
    int rem;     /* The remainder */
} div_t;
```

Syntax

```
#include <stdlib.h>
div_t div(int numer, int denom);
int numer;                    Numerator
int denom;                    Denominator
```

Example Use

```
result = div(32, 5);
/* result.quot = 6 and result.rem = 2 */
```

Returns

The *div* function returns a structure of type *div_t* containing the quotient and remainder of the division.

See Also

ldiv, div_t

div_t

Purpose

The *div_t* data type can hold the value returned by the *div* function. It is defined in STDLIB.H.

See Also

div

do

Purpose

Use the *do* keyword with *while* to form iterative loops where the statement or statements in the body are executed until the expression evaluates to 0 (false). The expression is evaluated after each execution of the loop body. Note that a *do...while* statement is always executed at least once. Since the entire *do...while* statement counts as a statement it must end with a semicolon.

Syntax

```
do
{
    statement;
    ...
};
```

```
while(condition);
/* if there is only one statement in the body
   the loop can be written:
   do statement while (condition); */
```

Example Use

```
do
{
    sum += i;
    i++;
}
while(i >= 10);
```

See Also

```
for, if, while
```

double

Purpose

Use the *double* type specifier to declare double precision floating point variables and arrays. In most implementations the *double* type is stored in twice as many bytes as *float*, though this is not required by the ANSI standard.

Syntax

```
double <varname>;
```

Example Use

```
/* declare a double, a pointer to a
   double, and an array of doubles */
   double d, *p_d, dvars[80];
```

See Also

```
char, float, int, long, short, signed, unsigned
```

EDOM

Purpose

The *EDOM* constant indicates an invalid argument (or "domain") error. It is defined in ERRNO.H.

See Also

```
ERANGE
```

elif preprocessor else-if operator

Purpose
Use the *#elif* operator to specify an alternate branch for conditional compilation.

Syntax
See *#if*

Example Use
See *#if*

See Also
`#if, #else, #endif`

else

Purpose
Use the *else* keyword as part of an *if* statement when you want to specify statements to be executed if the condition is false (0). When *if...else* statements are "nested" a particular *else* is always associated with the first preceding *if* that does not have an *else.*

Syntax
```
if (condition)
     statement_1;
else
         statement_2;
```

where *statement_1* is executed if the *expression* is not equal to zero, otherwise *statement_2* is executed.

Example Use
See *if* for an example.

See Also
`if, default, #else (preprocessor else operator)`

#else

Purpose
Use the *#else* operator to specify an alternate branch for conditional compilation.

Syntax
See *#if*

Example Use
See *#if*

See Also
`#if, #elif, #endif`

#endif preprocessor operator

Purpose
Use the *#endif* preprocessor operator to mark the end of an *#if* preprocessor directive.

Syntax
See *#if*

Example Use
See *#if*

See Also
`#if, #else, #elif`

enum

Purpose
Use the *enum* keyword to define a set of related values, often values that are considered to be in a particular order. This is an integral data type that can take its values from a list of enumerated constants.

Syntax
```
/* declare an enumerated type & a list of values */
enum identifier { enumerated_list };
/* declare two variables to be of this type */
enum identifier var1, var2;
```

Example Use
```
/* make traffic_signal the name of an
   enumerated type, with the values red, yellow, and
   green */
enum traffic_signal {red = 10, yellow = 20, green =
30};
/* declare signal_1 to be a variable of
   the traffic_signal type and p_signal to be a
   pointer to data of the traffic_signal type */
enum traffic_signal signal_1, *p_signal;
```

See Also

```
typedef
```

EOF

Purpose

The *EOF* negative integer constant indicates "end-of-file." It usually has a value of -1, and is defined in STDIO.H.

errno

Purpose

The *errno* predefined variable is a code indicating the last error that has occurred. It is defined in ERRNO.H.

See Also

```
perror
```

#error preprocessor operator

Purpose

Use the *#error* preprocessor operator to produce a diagnostic message during compilation.

Syntax

```
#error <message text>
```

Example Use

```
#if defined(WRONG_OPTION)
    #error Recompile with correct option
#endif
```

See Also

```
#if, #else, #elif, #endif, defined
```

exit

Purpose

Use *exit* to terminate your program normally by flushing file buffers, closing files, and invoking functions set up with *atexit.* A value of 0 or EXIT_SUCCESS for *status* means normal exit, whereas the value of EXIT_FAILURE is used to indicate errors.

Syntax

```
#include <stdlib.h>
```

```
void exit(int status);
int status;                         Exit status code
```

Example Use

```
exit(EXIT_SUCCESS);
```

See Also

abort, atexit, EXIT_FAILURE, EXIT_SUCCESS

EXIT_FAILURE

Purpose

The *EXIT_FAILURE* status code can be used with *exit* to indicate that the program ended with an error. It is defined in STDDEF.H.

See Also

EXIT_SUCCESS

EXIT_SUCCESS

Purpose

The *EXIT_SUCCESS* status code can be used with *exit* to indicate that the program executed successfully. It is defined in STDDEF.H.

See Also

EXIT_FAILURE

exp

Purpose

Use the *exp* function to compute the exponential of the *double* variable *x*. The exponential of a variable *x* is e^x where *e* is the base of natural logarithm ($e = 2.7182818$).

Syntax

```
#include <math.h>
double exp(double x);
double x;              Variable whose exponential is to be computed
```

Example Use

```
y = exp(x);
```

Returns

Normally, *exp* returns the exponential of *x*. If the value of the result is too large, a range error occurs.

See Also

`log`

extern

Purpose

Use the *extern* keyword to tell the compiler that a variable or a function is defined in another module (a separate file) and that you want to use it in the current module. The data item or function must be declared in one of the program modules without the *static* or the *extern* qualifier.

Syntax

```
extern <type> <varname>
```

Example Use

```
/* In the example below the variables current_state
   and state_table are shared among FILE 1 and FILE
   2.They are defined in FILE 1, and declared to be
   extern in FILE 2 */

/* FILE1 */
int current_state, state_table[MAXSTATE][MAXSYMB];

/* following is reference to variable declared in
   file2 */
   extern void next_state(int in_symbol);
main()
{
  int in_symbol;
  :
  current_state = 0;
  next_state(in_symbol);
  :
}

/*  FILE2 */
void next_state(int in_symbol)
{
   /* following declaration is referenced in file1 */
   extern int current_state,state_table[MAXSTATE]
   [MAXSYMB];
```

```
    if ( current_state == 0 ) ...
    :
    current_state = state_table[current_state]
    [in_symbol];
    :
}
```

See Also

`static`

\f escape sequence for form feed

Purpose

Use the *\f* (form feed) escape sequence to start a new page on the printer. On most systems the form feed displays as a single character rather than affecting the screen display.

Example Use

```
printf("%s", footer);
printf("\f"); /* start a new page */
printf("%s", header);
```

See Also

`printf`

fabs

Purpose

Use the *fabs* function to obtain the absolute value of its argument, which must be a double value.

Syntax

```
#include <math.h>
double fabs(double x);
double x;            Variable whose absolute value is to be returned
```

Example Use

```
y = fabs(-5.15); /* y will be 5.15 */
```

Returns

The return value is of type *double* with a positive value which is the absolute value of *x*.

See Also

`abs`

fclose

Purpose

Use *fclose* to close the stream specified by *stream.* If the stream was open for writing, the contents of the buffer associated with the stream is written to the file ("flushed") before the file is closed. If it was open for reading, any unread data in the buffer are discarded.

Syntax

```
#include <stdio.h>
int fclose(FILE *stream);
FILE *stream;                    Pointer to stream to be closed
```

Example Use

```
fclose(infile);
```

Returns

fclose returns 0 if the stream was successfully closed; otherwise, it returns EOF.

See Also

`fopen, fflush, EOF, FILE`

feof

Purpose

Use *feof* to determine whether *stream*'s end-of-file indicator is set. When you get an error return from a read operation, you can call *feof* to determine if the error occurred because you tried to read past the end-of-file.

Syntax

```
#include <stdio.h>
int feof(FILE *stream);
FILE *stream;          Pointer to FILE data structure associated with the stream
                       whose status is being checked
```

Example Use

```
if (feof(infile) != 0) printf("File ended\n");
```

Returns

feof returns a non-zero if and only if the end-of-file indicator is set for *stream.*

See Also

`clearerr, ferror, rewind, FILE`

ferror

Purpose

Use *ferror* to determine if the error indicator is set for the specified *stream.*

Syntax

```
#include <stdio.h>
int ferror(FILE *stream);
FILE *stream;                Pointer to FILE data structure associated
                             with the stream whose status is being checked
```

Example Use

```
if (ferror(infile) != 0) printf("Error detected\n");
```

Returns

ferror returns a non-zero value if and only if the error indicator is set for *stream.*

See Also

clearerr, feof, FILE

fflush

Purpose

Use the *fflush* function to flush the current contents of the buffer associated with the stream specified by *stream.* If the file is open for write operations, the "flushing" involves writing the contents of the buffer to the file. Otherwise, the buffer is cleared. If *stream* is NULL, the flushing action is performed on all open streams.

Syntax

```
#include <stdio.h>
int fflush(FILE *stream);
FILE *stream;          Pointer to stream whose buffer is being flushed
```

Example Use

```
fflush(stdin);
```

Returns

If the flushing is successful, *fflush* returns a 0. In case of an error, it returns the constant EOF defined in *stdio.h.*

See Also

fopen, fclose, setbuf, setvbuf, EOF, FILE, NULL

fgetc

Purpose

Use *fgetc* to read a single character from the stream specifed by the pointer *stream.* The character is read from the current position in the stream. After reading the character, the current position is advanced to the next character.

Syntax

```
#include <stdio.h>
int fgetc(FILE *stream);
FILE *stream;          Pointer to stream from which a character is to be read
```

Example Use

```
char_read = fgetc(infile);
```

Returns

If there are no errors, *fgetc* returns the character read, as an *unsigned char* converted to an *int*. Otherwise, it returns the constant EOF. You should call *ferror* and *feof* to determine if there really was an error or the file simply reached its end.

See Also

```
getc, getchar, fputc, putc, putchar, EOF, FILE, stdin
```

fgetpos

Purpose

Use *fgetpos* to get and save the current position indicator of the stream specified by the argument *stream* in the *fpos_t* data object *current_pos.* This value can be used only by the companion function *fsetpos* to reposition the stream to its position at the time of the call to *fgetpos.*

Syntax

```
#include <stdio.h>
int fgetpos(FILE *stream, fpos_t *current_pos);
FILE *stream;          Pointer to stream whose current position is requested
fpos_t *current_pos;   Pointer to variable where file's current position
                       is returned
```

Example Use

```
fgetpos(infile, &curpos);
```

Returns

If successful, *fgetpos* returns a 0. In case of error, it returns a non-zero value and sets the global variable *errno* to an implementation-defined error constant.

See Also

```
fsetpos, errno, fpos_t
```

fgets

Purpose

Use the *fgets* function to read a line from the stream specified by *stream.* The line is read into the character array *string* until a new-line ('\n') character is encountered, an end-of-file condition occurs, or the number of characters read reaches one less than the value given in the argument *maxchar.* A null character is written to *string* immediately after the last character.

Syntax

```
#include <stdio.h>
char *fgets(char *string, int maxchar, FILE *stream);
char *string;         Pointer to buffer where characters will be stored
int maxchar;          Maximum number of characters that can be stored
FILE *stream;         Pointer to stream from which a line is read
```

Example Use

```
fgets(buffer, 80, infile);
```

Returns

If there are no errors, *fgets* returns the argument *string.* Otherwise, it returns a NULL. You can call *ferror* and *feof* to determine whether the error is a genuine one or it occurred because the file reached its end.

See Also

```
gets, fputs, puts, FILE, NULL
```

FILE (data type)

Purpose

The *FILE* data type contains the information needed to perform file I/O. It is defined in STDIO.H.

See Also

EOF, FILENAME_MAX

__FILE__ predefined macro

Purpose

Use the *__FILE__* predefined macro to display the name of the source file being translated by the preprocessor.

Example Use

```
printf("Now preprocessing: ");
printf(__FILE__);
```

See Also

__DATE__, __TIME__, __LINE__, __STDC__

FILENAME_MAX

Purpose

The *FILENAME_MAX* predefined value gives the maximum length of a file name string, and is dependent on the operating system in use. It is defined in STDIO.H.

See Also

FILE

float

Purpose

Use the *float* data type specifier to declare single precision floating point variables and arrays.

Syntax

```
float <varname>
```

Example Use

```
/* declare a float, a pointer to a
   float, and an array of float */
float f, *p_f, fvars[100];
```

See Also

char, double, int, long, short, signed, unsigned

floor

Purpose

Use the *floor* function to get the "floor" of a *double* argument *x*. The "floor" is the largest integral value that is less than or equal to *x*. This can be used in rounding a *double down* to the preceding integer.

Syntax

```
#include <math.h>
double floor(double x);
double x;                    Variable whose "floor" is to be returned
```

Example Use

```
x = floor(4.15);  /* x will be 4.0 */
```

Returns

The return value is the "floor" of *x* expressed as a *double.*

See Also

`ceil`

FLT_DIG

Purpose

The *FLT_DIG* predefined value gives the number of significant decimal digits in a *float* value. It is defined in FLOAT.H.

See Also

`FLT_EPSILON, FLT_MANT_DIG, FLT_MIN, FLT_MIN_10_EXP, FLT_MIN_EXP, FLT_MAX, FLT_MAX_10_EXP, FLT_MAX_EXP, FLT_RADIX`

FLT_EPSILON

Purpose

The *FLT_EPSILON* predefined value gives the smallest positive *float* value *x* such that *1+x != 1.* It is defined in FLOAT.H.

See Also

`FLT_DIG, FLT_MANT_DIG, FLT_MIN, FLT_MIN_10_EXP, FLT_MIN_EXP, FLT_MAX, FLT_MAX_10_EXP, FLT_MAX_EXP, FLT_RADIX`

FLT_MANT_DIG

Purpose

The *FLT_MANT_DIG* predefined value gives the number of base *FLT_RADIX* digits in the mantissa of a *float.* It is defined in FLOAT.H.

See Also

`FLT_DIG, FLT_EPSILON, FLT_MIN, FLT_MIN_10_EXP, FLT_MIN_10, FLT_MAX, FLT_MAX_10_EXP, FLT_MAX_EXP, FLT_RADIX`

FLT_MAX

Purpose

The *FLT_MAX* predefined value gives the maximum representable finite value that can be stored in a *float.* It is defined in FLOAT.H.

See Also

FLT_DIG, FLT_MANT_DIG, FLT_EPSILON, FLT_MIN, FLT_MIN_10_EXP, FLT_MIN_10, FLT_MAX_10_EXP, FLT_MAX_EXP, FLT_RADIX

FLT_MAX_10_EXP

Purpose

The *FLT_MAX_10_EXP* predefined value gives the maximum integer such that 10 raised to that power is representable in a *float.*

See Also

FLT_DIG, FLT_MANT_DIG, FLT_EPSILON, FLT_MIN, FLT_MIN_10_EXP, FLT_MIN_EXP, FLT_MAX, FLT_MAX_EXP, FLT_RADIX

FLT_MAX_EXP

Purpose

The *FLT_MAX_EXP* predefined value gives the maximum integer such that FLT_RADIX raised to that power is representable in a *float.* It is defined in FLOAT.H.

See Also

FLT_DIG, FLT_MANT_DIG, FLT_EPSILON, FLT_MIN, FLT_MIN_10_EXP, FLT_MIN_EXP, FLT_MAX, FLT_MAX_10_EXP, FLT_RADIX

FLT_MIN

Purpose

The *FLT_MIN* predefined value gives the minimum positive floating-point number that can be stored in a *float.* It is defined in FLOAT.H.

See Also

FLT_DIG, FLT_MANT_DIG, FLT_EPSILON, FLT_MIN_10_EXP, FLT_MIN_EXP, FLT_MAX, FLT_MAX_10_EXP, FLT_MAX_EXP, FLT_RADIX

FLT_MIN_10_EXP

Purpose

The *FLT_MIN_10_EXP* predefined value gives the minimum negative integer such that 10 raised to that power is representable in a *float*. It is defined in FLOAT.H.

See Also

FLT_DIG, FLT_MANT_DIG, FLT_EPSILON, FLT_MIN, FLT_MIN_EXP, FLT_MAX, FLT_MAX_10_EXP, FLT_MAX_EXP, FLT_RADIX

FLT_MIN_EXP

Purpose

The *FLT_MIN_EXP* predefined value gives the minimum negative integer such that FLT_RADIX raised to that power minus 1 is representable in a *float*.

See Also

FLT_DIG, FLT_MANT_DIG, FLT_EPSILON, FLT_MIN, FLT_MIN_10_EXP, FLT_MAX, FLT_MAX_10_EXP, FLT_MAX_EXP, FLT_RADIX

FLT_RADIX

Purpose

The *FLT_RADIX* predefined value gives the radix of the exponent used for numeric representation (usually 2 for binary exponent). It is defined in FLOAT.H.

See Also

FLT_DIG, FLT_MANT_DIG, FLT_EPSILON, FLT_MIN, FLT_MIN_EXP, FLT_MIN_10_EXP, FLT_MAX, FLT_MAX_10_EXP, FLT_MAX_EXP

FLT_ROUNDS

Purpose

The *FLT_ROUNDS* predefined value gives a constant that indicates how floating-point values are rounded. The possible values are -1 (indeterminate), 0 (towards 0), 1 (to nearest representable value), 2 (towards positive infinity), and 3 (towards negative infinity). It is defined in FLOAT.H.

See Also

`FLT_DIG, FLT_MANT_DIG, FLT_EPSILON, FLT_MIN, FLT_MIN_EXP, FLT_MIN_10_EXP, FLT_MAX, FLT_MAX_10_EXP, FLT_MAX_EXP, FLT_RADIX`

fmod

Purpose

Use the *fmod* function to compute the floating-point remainder after dividing the floating-point number *x* by *y* and ensuring that the quotient is the largest possible integral value. If this quotient is *n*, then *fmod* returns the value *r* computed from the expression r = x - n*y. The entire operation is equivalent to:

```
double n, r;
:
:
n = floor(x/y);
r = x - n*y;
```

Syntax

```
#include <math.h>
double fmod(double x, double y);
double x, y;          The remainder after the division x/y is returned
```

Example Use

```
rem = fmod(24.95, 5.5); /* rem will be 2.95 */
```

Returns

When *y* is zero, *fmod* returns a zero. Otherwise, it returns the remainder computed as described above.

See Also

`floor`

fopen

Purpose

Use *fopen* to open the file whose name is in the string *filename* and associate a stream with it. The argument *access_mode* contains one of the following strings

Access_mode	Intrepretation
"r"	Open a text file for reading. Fail if file does not exist.
"w"	If file exists, open and truncate it to zero length. Otherwise create the file and open it for writing in the text mode.
"a"	Open text file for appending—writing at the end of file. Create file if it does not already exist.
"rb"	Same as "r" — but binary mode.
"wb"	Same as "w" — but binary mode.
"ab"	Same as "a" — but binary mode.
"r+"	Open text file for updating—reading as well as writing.
"w+"	If file exists, open it and truncate it to zero length. Otherwise, create it and open it for updating.
"a+"	Open text file for appending. Create file if it does not already exist.
"r+b" or "rb+"	Open binary file for updating.
"w+b" or "wb+"	If file exists, truncate to zero length; else create a binary file for update operations.
"a+b" or "ab+"	Open or create binary file for appending.

Syntax

```
#include <stdio.h>
FILE *fopen(const char *filename, const char
*access_mode);
const char *filename;      Name of file to be opened
const char *access_mode;   A character string denoting whether file is being
                           opened for read, write or append
```

Example Use

```
input_file = fopen("data.in", "rb");
```

Returns

If the file is successfully opened, *fopen* returns a pointer to the FILE data structure that controls the stream. The FILE structure is allocated elsewhere and you do not have to allocate it. In case of an error, *fopen* returns NULL.

See Also

```
fclose, freopen, setbuf, setvbuf, FILE, NULL
```

FOPEN_MAX

Purpose

The *FOPEN_MAX* predefined value gives the minimum number of files that can be open simultaneously. It is defined in STDIO.H.

See Also

```
BUFSIZ, FILENAME_MAX
```

for

Purpose

Use the *for* keyword to create a loop that will be executed for a specified number of times. Usually an index variable is set to a starting value and progressively varied each time the body of the loop is executed. The index variable is compared to a specified condition before each execution of the loop body: when the condition is satisfied (evaluates as 1 or true) the body of the loop is not executed and control resumes with the statement following the end of the loop.

Syntax

```
for (initialization; condition; varying) statement;
```

where the *initialization* is evaluated once at the beginning of the loop, and the *varying statement* is executed until the *condition* evaluates to 0 (false). The statement for varying the loop index is evaluated after each execution of *statement.*

Example Use

```
/* add the numbers from 1 to limit, all inside
   the loop specifications */

for(i=0, sum=0; i <= limit; sum += i, i++);
printf("\nSum from 1 to %d = %d\n", limit, sum);
```

Notice that there can be more than one statement in each part of the loop specification, with successive statements in a group being separated with commas. Here the initialization is *i = 0, sum = 0;* and the varying statements are *sum += i, i ++.*

A *for* loop does not need to have a statement in the body; if the *printf* statement in the preceding example were omitted the loop would still function correctly and accumulate the sum.

See Also

```
break, continue, if, switch
```

fpos_t

Purpose

The *fpos_t* data type contains information enabling the specification of each unique position in a file. It is defined in STDIO.H.

See Also

```
fseek, ftell
```

fprintf

Purpose

Use the *fprintf* function to format and write character strings and values of C variables to the stream specified by the argument *stream.* See reference entry for *printf* for a description of the argument *format_string.*

Syntax

```
#include <stdio.h>
int fprintf(FILE *stream,const char *format_string,...);
FILE *stream;                 Pointer to stream to which the output goes
const char *format_string;    A character string which describes the
                              format to be used
...                           A variable number of arguments depending on the number of
                              items being printed
```

Example Use

```
fprintf(resultfile, "The result is %f\n", result);
```

Returns

The *fprintf* function returns the number of characters it has printed. In case of error, it returns a negative value.

See Also

```
printf, vfprintf, vprintf, sprintf, vsprintf, FILE
```

fputc

Purpose

Use *fputc* to write the single character *c* to the stream specified by *stream.*

Syntax

```
#include <stdio.h>
int fputc(int c, FILE *stream);
int c;                    Character to be written
FILE *stream;             Pointer to stream to which the character is to be written
```

Example Use

```
fputc('X', p_datafile);
```

Returns

If there are no errors, *fputc* returns the character written. Otherwise, it returns the constant EOF. You should call *ferror* to determine if there really was an error or the integer argument *c* just happened to be equal to EOF.

See Also

`fgetc, getc, getchar, putc, puts, EOF, FILE`

fputs

Purpose

Use the *fputs* function to write the C string given by *string* to the stream specified by *stream.*

Syntax

```
#include <stdio.h>
int fputs(const char *string, FILE *stream);
const char *string;       Null ('\0') terminated character string to be output
FILE *stream;             Pointer to stream to which the string is output
```

Example Use

```
fputs("Sample Input Data", p_datafile);
```

Returns

The *fputs* function returns a non-negative value if all goes well. In case of error, it returns the constant EOF.

See Also

`fgets, gets, puts, EOF, FILE`

fread

Purpose

Use the *fread* function to read the number of data items specified by *count*, each of size given by the argument *size*, from the current position in *stream*. The current position of *stream* is updated after the read.

Syntax

```
#include <stdio.h>
size_t fread(void *buffer, size_t size, size_t count,
                                    FILE *stream);
```

`void *buffer;`	*Pointer to buffer where* fread *will store the bytes it reads*
`size_t size;`	*Size in bytes of each data item*
`size_t count;`	*Maximum number of items to be read*
`FILE *stream;`	*Pointer to stream from which data items are to be read*

Example Use

```
numread = fread(buffer, sizeof(char), 80, infile);
```

Returns

The *fread* function returns the number of items it successfully read. If the return value is less than you expected, you can call *ferror* and *feof* to determine if a read error had occurred or if end-of-file has been reached.

See Also

`fopen, fwrite, fclose, FILE, size_t`

free

Purpose

Use the *free* function to deallocate (return to the pool of free memory) a block of memory which was allocated earlier by *malloc, calloc* or *realloc.* The address of the block is specified by the argument *mem_address* which is a pointer to the starting byte of the block. A NULL pointer argument is ignored by *free.*

Syntax

```
#include <stdlib.h>
void free(void *mem_address);
```

`void *mem_address;`	*Pointer to block of memory to be released*

Example Use

```
free(buffer);
```

See Also

`calloc, malloc, realloc, NULL`

freopen

Purpose

Use *freopen* to close *stream* and open another file whose name is in the string *filename* and attach *stream* to it. For example, you can use *freopen* to redirect I/O from the pre-opened file *stdout* to a file of your choice. See *fopen* for a description of the argument *access_mode*. The error indicator of *stream* will be cleared after the reopening.

Syntax

```
#include <stdio.h>
FILE *freopen(const char *filename, const char
       *access_mode, FILE *stream);
const char *filename;      Name of file to be reopened including drive and
                           directory specification
const char *access_mode;   A character string denoting whether file is being
                           reopened for read, write, or append
FILE *stream;              Pointer to stream to be reopened
```

Example Use

```
freopen("output.txt", "w", stdout);
/* Redirect stdout to a file */
```

Returns

If all goes well, *freopen* returns a pointer to the newly opened file. This returned pointer will be the same as the argument *stream*. In case of error, a NULL is returned.

See Also

```
fopen, fclose, FILE, NULL, stdout
```

frexp

Purpose

Use the *frexp* function to break down the floating-point number *x* into a mantissa *m* whose absolute value lies between 0.5 and 1.0, and an integer exponent *n*, so that $x = m\ 2^{n}$. The integer exponent *n* is stored by *frexp* in the location whose address is given in the argument *expptr*. If *x* is zero, the exponent will also be zero.

Syntax

```
#include <math.h>
double frexp(double x, int *expptr);
double x;          Floating-point argument to be decomposed
int *expptr;       Pointer to an integer where the exponent will be returned
```

Example Use

```
mantissa = frexp(5.1, &exponent);
/* mantissa will be 0.6375, exponent = 3 */
```

Returns

Normally *frexp* returns the mantissa *m* computed as described above. When *x* is zero, *frexp* returns a zero as the mantissa.

See Also

1dexp, modf

fscanf

Purpose

Use the *fscanf* function to read characters from *stream*, convert them to values according to format specifications embedded in the argument *format_string* and finally store the values into C variables whose addresses are provided in the variable length argument list. See *scanf* for more details on the argument *format_string*.

Syntax

```
#include <stdio.h>
int fscanf(FILE *stream, constchar *format_string,...);
FILE *stream;              Pointer to the stream from which reading will occur
const char *format_string;    A character string which describes the
                              format to be used
...                        Variable number of arguments representing addresses of
                           variables whose values are being read
```

Example Use

```
fscanf(infile, "Date: %d/%d/%d", &month, &day, &year);
```

Returns

The *fscanf* function returns the number of input items that were successfully read, converted and saved in variables. The count does not include items that were read and ignored. If an end-of-file is encountered during read, the return value will be equal to the constant EOF (defined in *stdio.h*).

See Also

scanf, sscanf, EOF, FILE

fseek

Purpose

Use the *fseek* function to reposition *stream* to the location specified by *offset* with respect to the argument *origin*. The valid values of *origin* are the following constants:

Origin	Interpretation of constant
SEEK_SET	Beginning of file
SEEK_CUR	Current position in the file
SEEK_END	End of file

Syntax

```
#include <stdio.h>
int fseek(FILE *stream, long offset, int origin);
FILE *stream;        Pointer to stream whose current position is to be set
long offset;         Offset of new position (in bytes) from origin
int origin;          A constant indicating the position from which to offset
```

Example Use

```
fseek(infile, 0L, SEEK_SET); /* Go to the beginning */
```

Returns

fseek returns a non-zero value only if it fails to position the stream.

See Also

fgetpos, fsetpos, ftell, FILE, SEEK_SET, SEEK_CUR, SEEK_END

fsetpos

Purpose

Use *fsetpos* to set the position where reading or writing will take place in *stream*. The new position is specified in a *fpos_t* data object whose address is in *current_pos*. For file position, you should use a value obtained by an earlier call to *fgetpos*.

Syntax

```
#include <stdio.h>
int fsetpos(FILE *stream, const fpos_t *current_pos);
FILE *stream;                  Pointer to stream whose current position is to be set
const fpos_t *current_pos;     Pointer to location containing new
                               value of file position
```

Example Use

```
fgetpos(infile, &curpos);
```

Returns

If successful, *fsetpos* clears the end-of-file indicator of *stream*, and returns zero. Otherwise, the return value will be non-zero and the global variable *errno* will be set to an implementation-defined error constant.

See Also

```
fgetpos, FILE, errno, fpos_t
```

ftell

Purpose

Use *ftell* to obtain the current position of *stream*. The position is expressed as a byte offset from the beginning of the file.

Syntax

```
#include <stdio.h>
long ftell(FILE *stream);
FILE *stream;          Pointer to stream whose current position is to be returned
```

Example Use

```
curpos = ftell(infile));
```

Returns

If successful, *ftell* returns a long integer containing the number of bytes the current position of *stream* is offset from the beginning of the file. In case of error, *ftell* returns -1L. Also, the global variable *errno* is set to an implementation-defined constant.

See Also

```
fgetpos, fseek, fsetpos, FILE, errno
```

fwrite

Purpose

Use the *fwrite* function to write the number of data items specified by *count*, each of size given by *size*, from *buffer* to the current position in *stream*. The current position of *stream* is updated after the write.

Syntax

```
#include <stdio.h>
size_t fwrite(const void *buffer, size_t size, size_t
                    count, FILE *stream);
```

```
const void *buffer;     Pointer to buffer in memory from where fwrite will get the
                        bytes it writes
size_t size;            Size in bytes of each data item
size_t count;           Maximum number of items to be written
FILE *stream;           Pointer to stream to which the data items are to be written
```

Example Use

```
numwrite = fwrite(buffer, sizeof(char), 80, outfile);
```

Returns

The *fwrite* function returns the number of items it actually wrote. If the return value is less than what you expect, an error may have occurred. Use *ferror* to verify this.

See Also

```
fopen, fread, fclose, FILE, size_t
```

getc

Purpose

Use the *getc* macro to read a single character from *stream*. *getc* is identical to *fgetc*, except that it is implemented as a macro. This means you should not provide it an argument that may cause any side effects.

Syntax

```
#include <stdio.h>
int getc(FILE *stream);
FILE *stream;        Pointer to stream from which a character is to read
```

Example Use

```
in_char = getc(p_txtfile);
```

Returns

The *getc* macro returns the character read as an integer value. A return value of EOF indicates an error.

See Also

```
fgetc, fputc, getchar, putc, putchar, EOF, FILE
```

getchar

Purpose

Use the *getchar* macro to read a single character from the pre-opened file *stdin* which is normally connected to your keyboard input. Note that *getchar* is identical to *getc* with *stream* set to *stdin*.

Syntax

```
#include <stdio.h>
int getchar(void);
```

Example Use

```
c = getchar();
```

Returns

The *getchar* macro returns the character read from *stdin* as an integer value. In case of any error the return value is equal to the constant EOF.

See Also

```
fgetc, fputc, getc, putc, putchar, EOF, stdin
```

getenv

Purpose

Use *getenv* to get the definition of the environment variable *varname* from the environment of the process.

Syntax

```
#include <stdlib.h>
char *getenv(const char *varname);
const char *varname;    Name of environment variable to look for
```

Example Use

```
current_path = getenv("PATH");
```

Returns

If *varname* is found, *getenv* returns a pointer to the string value of *varname.* If *varname* is undefined, *getenv* will return a NULL. Predefined environment variables vary with the operating system in use.

See Also

```
argc, argv
```

gets

Purpose

Use *gets* to read a line from the standard input file *stdin* into the string *buffer.* The reading continues until *gets* encounters a new-line character or end-of-file. At this point, it replaces the new-line character with a null character ('\0') and creates a C-style string. You must allocate room for the buffer in which the characters will be stored. Note that *fgets* performs similarly, but unlike *gets,* it retains the new-line character in the final string.

Syntax

```
#include <stdio.h>
char *gets(char *buffer);
char *buffer;                 Buffer where string will be stored
```

Example Use

```
gets(command_line);
```

Returns

If successful, *gets* returns *buffer*. Otherwise, it returns a NULL.

See Also

```
fgets, fputs, puts, NULL, stdin
```

gmtime

Purpose

Use the *gmtime* function to break down a time value of type *time_t* stored at the location *time* into year, month, day, hour, minutes, seconds, and several other fields that it saves in a structure of type *tm* maintained internally. The structure *tm* is defined in *time.h* and shown in the entry for *asctime*. The fields setting up *gmtime* will correspond to Greenwich Mean Time (GMT).

Syntax

```
#include <time.h>
struct tm *gmtime(const time_t *time);
const time_t *time;           Pointer to calendar time
```

Example Use

```
t_gmt = gmtime(&bintime);
```

Returns

The *gmtime* function returns a pointer to the *tm* structure where the converted time is stored. If GMT is not available, it returns a NULL.

See Also

```
asctime, localtime, time, NULL, time_t, tm
```

goto

Purpose

Use the *goto* keyword to jump unconditionally to a label in the current function. The label ends in a colon. If the *goto* is executed, control jumps to the code following the specified label.

Use of *goto* is not recommended for most applications because it makes it hard to follow the flow of execution in the program.

Syntax

```
goto <label>;
```

Example Use

```
if (system_price > 6000.0) goto TooExpensive;
    :
TooExpensive:
    seek_alternative();
```

HUGE_VAL

Purpose

The value *HUGE_VAL* is a predefined *double* expression that evaluates to a very large value (for use as return value by math functions when the computed result is too large). It is defined in MATH.H.

See Also

```
INT_MAX, DBL_MAX, FLT_MAX
```

if

Purpose

Use *if* to execute code only when certain conditions hold true. You can use *if* alone or with *else* to specify multiple alternatives.

Syntax

```
if (<condition>)
        <statement; ...>
```

or

```
if (<condition>)
        statement_1
else
        statement_2;
```

The statement following the *if* is executed if the *condition* is true (not equal to 0). When an *else* is present, statement_2 is executed if *condition* is false (equal to 0).

Example Use

```
:if ( x <= y)  smaller = x;
else smaller = y;
:
```

If *x* is less than or equal to *y*, then *smaller* is assigned the value *x*. Otherwise (else), *smaller* is assigned the value *y*.

See Also

`else`

#if preprocessor conditional directive

Purpose

Use the *#if* preprocessor directive to control what parts of your code will be compiled under which conditions.

Syntax

```
#if <condition>
    <directive1>
#elif <condition2>
    <directive2>
...
#else
    <default_directive>
#endif
```

If *condition1* is true, *directive1* is executed by the preprocessor, otherwise if *condition2* is true, *directive2* is executed. If neither *condition1* nor *condition2* are true, then *default_directive* is executed. You can have no *#elif* or more than one of them; you can omit *#else* but not have more than one *#else*.

Example Use

```
#if !defined(FILE_1_INCLUDED)
    #include <file1.h>
#elif defined(INCLUDE_FILE_2)
    #include <file2.h>
#else
    #include <file3.h>
#endif
```

See Also

`defined (preprocessor condition), #include`

#ifdef preprocessor operator

Purpose

Use the *#ifdef* preprocessor operator to determine whether a preprocessor symbol or macro is defined in the current program. The *#ifdef* operator is equivalent to *#if defined.*

Syntax

```
#ifdef (SYMBOL)
```

Example Use

```
#ifdef (NON_STANDARD)
        #include "ourdefs.h"
#endif
```

See Also

defined (preprocessor operator), #ifndef

#ifndef

Purpose

Use the *#ifndef* preprocessor operator to determine whether a preprocessor symbol or macro is defined in the current program. *#ifndef* is equivalent to *#if !defined.*

Syntax

```
#ifndef (SYMBOL)
```

Example Use

```
#ifndef (COPROCESSOR)
        #include "emulate.h"
#endif
```

See Also

defined (preprocessor operator), #idef

#include preprocessor directive

Purpose

Use the *#include* preprocessor directive to have the preprocessor read a header file (sometimes called an "include file") into the source code. The contents of the included file will be compiled along with the original source file.

Syntax

```
#include <filename>        /* read file from default
                              directory */
#include "filename"        /* read file from same
                              directory as source
                              code—details vary with
                              implementation */
```

Example Use

```
#include <stdio.h>
```

int

Purpose

Use the *int* type specifier to declare integer variables and arrays. The size qualifiers *short* and *long* should be used to declare an integer of desired size. The size of an *int* is implementation-dependent.

Syntax

```
int <varname>;
```

Example Use

```
int i, x[100];
```

See Also

```
char, double, float, long, short, signed, unsigned
```

INT_MAX

Purpose

The predefined value *INT_MAX* is the maximum value of an *int.* It is defined in LIMITS.H.

See Also

```
HUGE_VAL, DBL_MAX, FLT_MAX
```

INT_MIN

Purpose

The predefined value *INT_MIN* is the minimum value of an *int.* It is defined in LIMITS.H.

See Also

```
DBL_MIN, FLT_MIN
```

_IOFBF

Purpose

The predefined value *_IOFBF* indicates "full buffering" when used with *setvbuf.* It is defined in STDIO.H.

See Also

`_IOLBF, _IONBF, setvbf`

_IOLBF

Purpose

The predefined value *_IOLBF* indicates "line buffering" when used with *setvbuf.* It is defined in STDIO.H.

See Also

`_IOFBF, _IONBF, setvbf`

_IONBF

Purpose

The predefined value *_IONBF* indicates "line buffering" when used with *setvbuf.* It is defined in STDIO.H.

See Also

`IOFBF, _IOLBF, setvbf`

isalnum

Purpose

Use *isalnum* function to check if the character *c* is alphanumeric. It is equivalent to testing if *isalpha* or *isdigit* is true for *c.*

Syntax

```
#include <ctype.h>
int isalnum(int c);
int c;                  Character being tested
```

Example Use

```
if(isalnum(c) != 0) printf("%c is alphanumeric\n", c);
```

Returns

The *isalnum* function returns a non-zero value if the *c* is indeed an alphanumeric character. Otherwise it returns a zero.

See Also

`isalpha, isdigit`

isalpha

Purpose

Use *isalpha* function to check if the character *c* is either a lowercase or an uppercase letter. If the locale is not "C", the behavior is dependent upon the character set in use.

Syntax

```
#include <ctype.h>
int isalpha(int c);
int c;                                    Character being tested
```

Example Use

```
if(isalpha(c) != 0) printf("%c is letter\n", c);
```

Returns

The *isalpha* function returns a non-zero value if *c* is a letter. Otherwise it returns a zero.

See Also

```
islower, isupper, setlocale
```

iscntrl, isdigit, isgraph, islower, isprint, ispunct, isspace, isupper, isxdigit

Purpose

Use this group of functions to check for specific properties of the character *c* such as whether it is a control character, a digit, lowercase, printable, and so on. The table below shows the test performed by each of the functions.

Function name	Tests for
iscntrl	control character
isdigit	decimal digit
isgraph	printable character excluding the space
islower	lowercase letter
isprint	printable character including space
ispunct	punctuation character
isspace	"whitespace" character (in "C" locale these are space, formfeed '\f', new-line '\n', carriage return '\r', horizontal tab '\t', and vertical tab '\v')
isupper	uppercase letter
isxdigit	hexadecimal digit

Syntax

```
#include <ctype.h>
int iscntrl(int c);
int isdigit(int c);
int isgraph(int c);
int islower(int c);
int isprint(int c);
int ispunct(int c);
int isspace(int c);
int isupper(int c);
int isxdigit(int c);
int c;                    Character to be tested
```

Example Use

```
if(isprint(c) != 0) printf("%c is printable\n", c);
if(isdigit(c) != 0) printf("%c is a digit\n", c);
if(iscntrl(c) != 0) printf("%d is a control char\n", c);
```

Returns

Each function returns a non-zero value if the *c* satisfies the criterion for that function. Otherwise it returns a zero.

See Also

`isalnum, isalpha`

jmp_buf

Purpose

The *jmp_buf* array type is capable of holding information necessary to restore a calling environment. It is defined in SETJMP.H.

See Also

`longjmp, setjmp`

L_tmpnam

Purpose

The predefined value *L_tmpnam* is the size of a char array large enough to hold temporary file names generated by tmpnam. It is defined in STDIO.H.

See Also

`tmpnam, FILENAME_MAX`

LC_ALL

Purpose

The predefined constant *LC ALL* indicates the program's entire locale (aspects that depend on country-specific formats). It is defined in LOCALE.H.

See Also

`LC_COLLATE, LC_CTYPE, LC_MONETARY, LC_NUMERIC, LC_TIME`

labs

Purpose

Use *labs* to get the absolute value of the long integer n.

Syntax

```
#include <stdlib.h>
long labs(long n);
long n;                 Long integer whose absolute value is returned
```

Example Use

```
lresult = labs(-65540L); /* result will be 65540 */
```

Returns

The long integer returned by *labs* is the absolute value of *n*.

See Also

`abs, fabs`

LC_COLLATE

Purpose

The predefined constant *LC_COLLATE* affects the behavior of *strcoll* and *strxfrm*. It is defined in LOCALE.H.

See Also

`LC_ALL, LC_CTYPE, LC_MONETARY, LC_NUMERIC, LC_TIME, strcoll, strxfrm`

LC_CTYPE

Purpose

The predefined constant *LC_CTYPE* affects the behavior of all locale-aware character handling routines. It is defined in LOCALE.H.

See Also

`LC_ALL, LC_COLLATE, LC_MONETARY, LC_NUMERIC, LC_TIME,`

LC_MONETARY

Purpose

The predefined constant *LC_MONETARY* affects monetary formatting information returned by *localeconv*. It is defined in LOCALE.H.

See Also

`LC_ALL, LC_COLLATE, LC_CTYPE, LC_NUMERIC, LC_TIME`
`localeconv`

LC_NUMERIC

Purpose

The predefined constant *LC_NUMERIC* affects the locale-specific decimal point formatting information returned by *localeconv*. It is defined in LOCALE.H.

See Also

`LC_ALL, LC_COLLATE, LC_CTYPE, LC_TIME, LC_MONETARY,`
`localeconv`

LC_TIME

Purpose

The predefined constant *LC_TIME* affects the behavior of the *strftime* function. It is defined in LOCALE.H.

See Also

`LC_ALL, LC_COLLATE, LC_CTYPE, LC_NUMERIC,LC_MONETARY,`
`strftime`

lconv

Purpose

The *lconv* struct holds strings to be used in formatting numeric and monetary values for a specified locale. It is defined in LOCALE.H.

See Also

`localeconv, LC_NUMERIC, LC_MONETARY`

LDBL_DIG

Purpose

The predefined value *LDBL_DIG* is the number of significant decimal digits in a *long double* value. It is defined in FLOAT.H.

See Also

LDBL_EPSILON, LDBL_MANT_DIG, LDBL_MIN, LDBL_MIN_10_EXP, LDBL_MIN_EXP, LDBL_MAX, LDBL_MAX_10_EXP, LDBL_MAX_EXP, LDBL_RADIX

LDBL_EPSILON

Purpose

The *LDBL_EPSILON* predefined value gives the smallest positive *long double* value *x* such that *1+x != 1.* It is defined in FLOAT.H.

See Also

LDBL_DIG, LDBL_MANT_DIG, LDBL_MIN, LDBL_MIN_10_EXP, LDBL_MIN_EXP, LDBL_MAX, LDBL_MAX_10_EXP,LDBL_MAX_EXP, LDBL_RADIX

LDBL_MANT_DIG

Purpose

The *LDBL_MANT_DIG* predefined value gives the number of base *IDBL_RADIX* digits in the mantissa of a *long double*. It is defined in FLOAT.H.

See Also

LDBL_DIG, LDBL_EPSILON, LDBL_MIN, LDBL_MIN_10_EXP, LDBL_MIN_10, LDBL_MAX, LDBL_MAX_10_EXP, LDBL_MAX_EXP, LDBL_RADIX

LDBL_MAX

Purpose

The *LDBL_MAX* predefined value gives the maximum representable finite value that can be stored in a *long double.* It is defined in FLOAT.H.

See Also

LDBL_DIG, LDBL_MANT_DIG, LDBL_EPSILON, LDBL_MIN, LDBL_MIN_10_EXP, LDBL_MIN_EXP LDBL_MAX_10_EXP, LDBL_MAX_EXP, LDBL_RADIX

LDBL_MAX_10_EXP

Purpose

The *LDBL_MAX_10_EXP* predefined value gives the maximum integer such that 10 raised to that power is representable in a *long double.*

See Also

`LDBL_DIG, LDBL_MANT_DIG, LDBL_EPSILON, LDBL_MIN, LDBL_MIN_10_EXP, LDBL_MIN_EXP, LDBL_MAX, LDBL_MAX_EXP, LDBL_RADIX`

LDBL_MAX_EXP

Purpose

The *LDBL_MAX_EXP* predefined value gives the maximum integer such that *LDBL_RADIX* raised to that power is representable in a *long double.* It is defined in FLOAT.H.

See Also

`LDBL_DIG, LDBL_MANT_DIG, LDBL_EPSILON, LDBL_MIN, LDBL_MIN_10_EXP, LDBL_MIN_EXP, LDBL_MAX, LDBL_MAX_10_EXP, LDBL_RADIX`

LDBL_MIN

Purpose

The *LDBL_MIN* predefined value gives the minimum positive long floating-point number that can be stored in a *long double.* It is defined in FLOAT.H.

See Also

`LDBL_DIG, LDBL_MANT_DIG, LDBL_EPSILON, LDBL_MIN_10_EXP, LDBL_MIN_EXP, LDBL_MAX, LDBL_MAX_10_EXP, LDBL_MAX_EXP, LDBL_RADIX`

LDBL_MIN_10_EXP

Purpose

The *LDBL_MIN_10_EXP* predefined value gives the minimum negative integer such that 10 raised to that power is representable in a *long double*. It is defined in FLOAT.H.

See Also

`LDBL_DIG, LDBL_MANT_DIG, LDBL_EPSILON, LDBL_MIN, LDBL_MIN_EXP, LDBL_MAX, LDBL_MAX_10_EXP, LDBL_MAX_EXP, LDBL_RADIX`

LDBL_MIN_EXP

Purpose

The *LDBL_MIN_EXP* predefined value gives the minimum negative integer such that LDBL_RADIX raised to that power minus 1 is representable in a *long double.* It is defined in FLOAT.H.

See Also

LDBL_DIG, LDBL_MANT_DIG, LDBL_EPSILON, LDBL_MIN, LDBL_MIN_10_EXP, LDBL_MAX, LDBL_MAX_10_EXP, LDBL_MAX_EXP, LDBL_RADIX

ldexp

Purpose

Use the *ldexp* function to compute and obtain the floating-point number equal to *x* times 2^{exp}.

Syntax

```
#include <math.h>
double ldexp(double x, int exp);
double x;              Floating-point value of the mantissa
int exp;               Integer exponent
```

Example Use

```
value = ldexp(0.6375, 3); /* value will be 5.1 */
```

Returns

Normally *ldexp* returns the value computed as described above. When the result is too large a range error may occur.

See Also

frexp, modf

ldiv

Purpose

Use the *ldiv* function to divide the long integer *numer* by another long integer *denom* and obtain the resulting quotient and remainder packed in a structure of type *ldiv_t*. The structure type *ldiv_t* is defined in *stdlib.h* as:

```
typedef struct
{
    long quot;   /* The quotient  */
    long rem;    /* The remainder */
} ldiv_t;
```

Syntax

```
#include <stdlib.h>
ldiv_t ldiv(long numer, long denom);
long numer;         Numerator
long denom;         Denominator
```

Example Use

```
lresult = ldiv(65540L, 65536L);
/* lresult.quot = 1, lresult.rem = 4 */
```

Returns

The *ldiv* function returns a structure of type *ldiv_t* containing the quotient and remainder of the division.

See Also

`div, ldiv_t`

ldiv_t

Purpose

The *ldiv_t* data type can hold the value returned by *ldiv.* It is defined in STDLIB.H.

See Also

`ldiv, div_t`

#line preprocessor line numbering directive

Purpose

Use the *#line* preprocessor to set the current line number for this location in the source code. This can be used as a debugging aid.

__LINE__ predefined macro

Purpose

Use the *__LINE__* predefined macro to display or check the number of the line currently being translated by the preprocessor.

Example Use

```
printf("%d", __LINE__);
```

See Also

`__DATE__, __TIME__, __FILE__, __STDC__`

localeconv

Purpose

Use the *localeconv* function to obtain detailed information on formatting monetary and numeric values according to the rules of the current locale. Note that many compilers support only the "C" locale at this time. The table below lists the categories of locale information that may be available.

Locale Category	Parts of Program Affected
LC_ALL	The entire program's locale-specific parts (all categories shown below).
LC_COLLATE	Behavior of the routines *strcoll* and *strxfrm*
LC_CTYPE	Behavior of the character handling functions and multibyte functions
LC_MONETARY	Monetary formatting information returned by the *ocaleconv* function.
LC_NUMERIC	Decimal point character for the formatted output routines (for example, *printf* and the data conversion functions, and the non-monetary formatting information returned by the *localeconv* function.
LC_TIME	Behavior of the *strftime* function

Syntax

```
#include <locale.h>
struct lconv *localeconv(void);
```

Example Use

```
p_lconv = localeconv();
```

Returns

The *localeconv* function returns a pointer to a statically allocated *lconv* structure whose fields are filled in with formatting information appropriate for the current locale. Use *setlocale* to set the current locale. The *lconv* structure is declared in *locale.h* as follows:

```
struct lconv
{
    char *decimal_point;    /* Decimal point
                               character for non-
                               monetary quantities */
    char *thousands_sep;    /* Separator for groups of
                               digits to the left of
                               decimal point for non-
                               monetary quantities */
    char *grouping;         /* Size of each group of
                               digits in non-monetary
                               quantities */
    char *int_curr_symbol; /* International currency
                               symbol for the current
                               locale */
    char *currency_symbol; /* Local currency symbol
                               for the current
                               locale */
    char *mon_decimal_point; /* Decimal  point char-
                               acter for monetary
                               quantities */
    char *mon_thousands_sep; /* Separator for groups
                               of digits to the left
                               of decimal point for
                               monetary quantities */
    char *mon_grouping;     /* Size of each group of
                               digits in monetary
                               quantities */
    char *positive_sign;    /* String denoting sign
                               for non-negative mone-
                               tary quantities */
    char *negative_sign;    /* String denoting sign
                               for negative monetary
                               quantities */
    char int_frac_digits;   /* Number of digits to the
                               right of decimal point
                               in internationally
                               formatted monetary
                               quantities */
```

```
    char frac_digits;      /* Number of digits to the
                              right of decimal point
                              in formatted monetary
                              quantities */
    char p_cs_precedes;    /* 1 = currency_symbol
                              precedes, 0 = succeeds
                              positive value */
    char p_sep_by_space;   /* 1 = space, 0 = no space
                              between currency_symbol
                              and positive formatted
                              values */
    char n_cs_precedes;    /* 1 = currency_symbol
                              precedes, 0 = succeeds
                              negative value */
    char n_sep_by_space;   /* 1 = space, 0 = no space
                              between currency_symbol
                              and negative formatted
                              values */
    char p_sign_posn;      /* Position of
                              positive_sign in
                              positive monetary
                              quantities */
    char n_sign_posn;      /* Position of
                              negative_sign in
                              negative monetary
                              quantities */
};
```

See Also

`setlocale, lconv`

localtime

Purpose

Use the *localtime* function to break down the value of time of type *time_t* stored at the location *time* into year, month, day, hour, minutes, seconds and several other fields that it saves in a structure of type *tm* maintained internally. The structure *tm* is defined in *time.h* and is shown in the reference pages on *asctime.* The fields set up by *localtime* will correspond to the local time.

Syntax

```
#include <time.h>
struct tm *localtime (const time_t *time);
const time_t *time;                    Pointer to stored calendar time
```

Example Use

```
t_local = localtime(&bintime);
```

Returns

The *localtime* function returns a pointer to the *tm* structure where the converted time is stored.

See Also

```
asctime, gmtime, time, time_t, tm
```

log, log10

Purpose

Use *log* and *log10* respectively to compute the natural logarithm and logarithm to the base 10 of the positive *double* variable *x*.

Syntax

```
#include <math.h>
double log(double x);
double log10(double x);
double x;                    Variable whose logarithm is to be computed
```

Example Use

```
y = log(2);     /* y = 0.693147 */
a = log10(2);   /* a = 0.30103  */
```

Returns

For positive *x*, *log* and *log10* returns the logarithm of *x*. If *x* is negative, a domain error occurs. If *x* is zero, a range error occurs.

See Also

```
exp, pow
```

long

Purpose

Use the *long* type specifier as a size qualifier for *int* and *unsigned int* variables. Note that *long* alone means *signed long int.* A *long* qualifier indicates that the integer data type is at least 32 bits, and is often twice as long as an *int.*

Example Use

```
long filepos; unsigned long timer_tick;
```

See Also

`char, double, float, int, short, signed, unsigned`

LONG_MAX

Purpose

The *LONG_MAX* predefined value is the maximum value of a *long int.* It is defined in LIMITS.H.

See Also

`LONG_MIN`

LONG_MIN

Purpose

The *LONG_MIN* predefined value is the minimum value of a *long int.* It is defined in LIMITS.H.

See Also

`LONG_MAX`

longjmp

Purpose

Use the *longjmp* function to restore the calling environment to that contained in the *jmp_buf* array *env.* This environment must have been saved by an earlier call to *setjmp. longjmp* restores all local variables (except the ones declared *volatile*) to their previous states and returns as if from the last call to *setjmp* with the return value *retval.*

Since *longjmp* jumps to the return address of the last matching call to *setjmp,* you must make sure that the call to *longjmp* occurs before the function where you had called *setjmp* has returned.

Syntax

```
#include <setjmp.h>
```

```
void longjmp(jmp_buf env, int retval);
jmp_buf env;              Array data type where the calling environment is stored
int retval;               Value that will appear to be returned by the earlier call to
                          setjmp
```

Example Use

```
longjmp(stack_env, 1);
```

See Also

setjmp, jmp_buf

malloc

Purpose

Use the *malloc* function to allocate the number of bytes requested in the argument *num_bytes.*

Syntax

```
#include <stdlib.h>
void *malloc(size_t num_bytes);
size_t num_bytes;              Number of bytes needed
```

Example Use

```
buffer = (char *)malloc(100*sizeof(char));
```

Returns

The *malloc* function returns a pointer which is the starting address of the memory allocated. If the memory allocation is unsuccessful because of insufficient space or bad values of the arguments, a NULL is returned.

See Also

free, calloc, realloc, NULL, size_t

MB_CUR_MAX

Purpose

The *MB_CUR_MAX* predefined value is the minimum value of a multibyte character for the current locale. It is defined in STDLIB.H, and is always less than *MB_LEN_MAX.*

See Also

MB_LEN_MAX

MB_LEN_MAX

Purpose

The *MB_LEN_MAX* predefined value is the maximum number of bytes in a multibyte character. It is defined in LIMITS.H.

See Also

`MB_CUR_MAX`

mblen

Purpose

Use the *mblen* function to obtain the number of bytes that makes up a single multibyte character. Note that some otherwise ANSI-compliant compilers do not support multibyte characters.

Syntax

```
#include <stdlib.h>
int mblen(const char *s, size_t n);
```

`const char *s;`	*Pointer to multibyte character whose length is to be determined*
`size_t n;`	*Maximum number of bytes expected to comprise a multibyte character (MB_CUR_MAX is a good choice for this argument)*

Example Use

```
mbsize = mblen(p_mbchar, MB_CUR_MAX);
```

Returns

If *s* is NULL, *mblen* returns a 0 or a non-zero depending on whether multibyte encodings have state dependencies or not. If *s* is not NULL, *mblen* returns the number of bytes that comprise the multibyte character provided the next *n* or fewer characters form a valid multibyte character. Otherwise, it returns -1.

See Also

`mbtowc, mbstowcs, wctomb, wcstombs, MB_CUR_MAX, NULL, size_t`

mbtowc

Purpose

Use the *mbtowc* function to convert a multibyte character at *s* to *wchar_t* type and store the result in the array *pwchar.* If *pwchar* is NULL, *mbtowc* will not save the resulting wide character. Also, *mbtowc* will check at most *n* characters in *s* when trying to locate a valid multibyte character.

Note that some otherwise ANSI-compliant compilers do not support multibyte characters.

Syntax

```
#include <stdlib.h>
int mbtowc(wchar_t *pwchar, const char *s, size_t n);
```

`wchar_t *pwchar;`	*Pointer to array where the wide character equivalent of multibyte character will be stored*
`const char *s;`	*Pointer to multibyte character to be converted to wide character format*
`size_t n;`	*Maximum number of bytes expected to comprise a multibyte character (MB_CUR_MAX is a good choice for this argument)*

Example Use

```
mdc_size = mbtowc(pwc, mbchar, MB_CUR_MAX);
```

Returns

If *s* is NULL, *mbtowc* will return a 0 or a non-zero depending on whether multibyte encodings have state dependencies or not. If *s* not NULL, *mbtowc* returns the number of bytes that comprise the multibyte character provided the next *n* or fewer characters form a valid multibyte character. Otherwise, it returns -1.

See Also

`mblen, mbstowcs, wctomb, wcstombs, MB_CUR_MAX, NULL, size_t, wchar_t`

mbstowcs

Purpose

Use the *mbstowcs* function to convert a sequence of multibyte characters in *mbs* into a sequence of codes of *wchar_t* type and stores at most *n* such codes in the array *pwcs*. Note that some otherwise ANSI-compliant compilers do not support multibyte characters.

Syntax

```
#include <stdlib.h>
size_t mbstowcs(wchar_t *pwcs, const char *mbs,
size_t n);
```

```
wchar_t *pwcs;        Pointer to array where wide character results will be stored
const char *mbs;      Pointer to array of multibyte characters being converted
                      to wide character

size_t  n;            Maximum number of wide characers to be stored in pwcs
```

Example Use

```
mbstowcs(wc_array, mb_array, 10);
```

Returns

If successful, *mbstowcs* returns the number of wide characters it stored in *pwcs.* If it encountered less than *n* multibyte characters, it returns -1 cast as *size_t.*

See Also

```
mblen, mbtowc, wctomb, wcstombs, size_t, wchar_t
```

memchr

Purpose

Use the *memchr* function to search through the first *count* bytes in the buffer at the address *buffer* and find the first occurrence of the character *c.*

Syntax

```
#include <string.h>
void *memchr(const void *buffer, int c, size_tcount);
const void *buffer;      Pointer to buffer in which search takes place

int c;                   Character to look for

size_t count;            Maximum number of bytes to be examined
```

Example Use

```
/* Look for the first occurrence of 'I' in a 100 byte
   buffer */

first_i = memchr(start_address, 'I', 100);
```

Returns

If *memchr* finds the character *c,* it will return a pointer to this character in *buffer.* Otherwise, *memchr* returns a NULL.

See Also

```
memcmp, strchr, NULL, size_t
```

memcmp

Purpose

Use the *memcmp* function to compare the first *count* bytes of the two buffers *buffer1, buffer2.*

Syntax

```
#include <string.h>
int memcmp(const void *buffer1, const void *buffer2,
size_t count);
const void *buffer1;        Pointer to first buffer
const void *buffer2;        Pointer to second buffer
size_t count;               Number of bytes to be compared
```

Example Use

```
if (memcmp(buffer1, buffer2, sizeof(buffer1)) == 0)
printf("The buffers are identical\n");
```

Returns

The *memcmp* function returns an integer less than, equal to, or greater than zero according to whether the string *buffer1* is less than, equal to, or greater than the string *buffer2.*

See Also

strcoll, strcmp, strncmp, size_t

memcpy

Purpose

Use the *memcpy* function to copy *count* bytes from the buffer at address *source* to another buffer at *dest.* The behavior of *memcpy* is undefined if the source and destination buffers overlap.

Syntax

```
#include <string.h>
void *memcpy(void *dest, const void *source, size_t
count);
void  *dest;              Pointer to buffer to which data will be copied
const void *source;       Pointer to buffer from which data will be copied
size_t  count;            Maximum number of bytes to be copied
```

Example Use

```
memcpy(dest, src, 80);    /* Copy 80 bytes from dest
                             to src */
```

Returns

The *memcpy* function returns a pointer to the destination buffer *dest.*

See Also

`memmove, strcpy, strncpy, size_t`

memmove

Purpose

Use the *memmove* function to copy *count* bytes from the buffer at address *source* to another buffer at *dest.* Parts of the source and destination buffers may overlap.

Syntax

```
#include <string.h>
void *memmove(void *dest, const void *source, size_t
count);
void *dest;                 Pointer to buffer to which data will be copied
const void  *source;        Pointer to buffer from which data will be copied
size_t  count;              Maximum number of bytes to be copied
```

Example Use

```
memmove(dest, src, sizeof(src));
```

Returns

The *memmove* function returns a pointer to the destination buffer *dest.*

See Also

`memcpy, strcpy, strncpy, size_t`

memset

Purpose

Use the *memset* function to set the first *count* bytes in the *buffer* to the character *c.*

Syntax

```
#include <string.h>
void *memset(void *buffer, int c, size_t count);
void *buffer;        Pointer to memory where bytes are to be set
int c;               Each byte in buffer will be set to this character
size_t count;        Maximum number of bytes to be set
```

Example Use

```
memset(big_buffer, '\0', 2048);
```

Returns

The *memset* function returns the argument *buffer.*

See Also

```
memcpy, memmove, strcpy, strncpy, size_t
```

mktime

Purpose

Use the *mktime* function to convert the local time currently in the structure of type *tm* at the address *timeptr* to a value of type *time_t.* Essentially, the local time given in the form of year, month, day etc. will be converted to number of seconds elapsed since 00:00:00 hours GMT, January 1, 1970. This is the same format in which *time* returns the current time and is the format used in the argument to the functions *ctime, difftime* and *localtime.*

Two fields in the structure of type *tm* are ignored by *mktime.* These are the fields *tm_wday* and *tm_yday,* denoting respectively the day of the week and the day of the year. The *mktime* function will set the fields in the *tm* structure to appropriate values before returning.

Syntax

```
#include <time.h>
time_t mktime(struct tm *timeptr);
struct tm *timeptr;
```

Pointer to structure of type tm *where local time is stored*

Example Use

```
bintime = mktime(&timebuf);
```

Returns

If successful, *mktime* will return the current contents of *timeptr* encoded as a value of type *time_t.* If the local time in *timeptr* can not be handled by *mktime,* the return value will be a -1 cast to the type *time_t.*

See Also

```
asctime, time, time_t, tm
```

modf

Purpose

Use the *modf* function to separate the floating-point number *x* into its fractional part and its integral part. The integer part is returned as a floating-point value in the location whose address is given in the argument *intptr*.

Syntax

```
#include <math.h>
double modf(double x, double *intptr);
double x;              Floating-point value to be decomposed
double *intptr;        Integral part of x is returned here
```

Example Use

```
fraction = modf(24.95, &int_part);
/* fraction is .95 */
```

Returns

The *modf* function returns the signed fractional part of *x*.

See Also

```
frexp, ldexp
```

\n escape sequence for new line

Purpose

Use the *\n* (new line) escape sequence to move the cursor or print head to the beginning of the next line. (The difference between *\r* (carriage return) and *\n* is that a carriage return moves the cursor or print head to the beginning of the *current* line.

Example Use

```
printf("This string is on one line\n");
printf("and this one goes on the next line.");
```

See Also

```
printf, \r
```

NDEBUG

Purpose

The *NDEBUG* value by default is not defined. If it is defined, *assert* will be ignored.

See Also

```
assert
```

NULL

Purpose

The value *NULL* indicates an implementation-defined null pointer constant. It is defined in LOCALE.H, STDDEF.H, STDIO.H, STDLIB.H, STRING.H, and TIME.H. This is more accurate than casting a pointer to a value of 0, which looks like an address, while NULL means "doesn't point to anything at all."

See Also

`* (pointer reference operator)`

offsetof

Purpose

The predefined *offsetof* macro has the form *offsetof(structure_type, member)* and returns a *size_t* value that is the offset in bytes, of the *member* from the beginning of a structure. It can be used to manipulate structure directly. It is defined in STDDEF.H.

See Also

`struct, union, . (member access operator),`
`-> (pointer member access operator)`

perror

Purpose

Use *perror* to construct an error message by concatenating your message provided in the argument *string* with that from the system message corresponding to the current value in the global variable *errno,* and print the message to *stderr.*

Syntax

```
#include <stdio.h>
void perror(const char *string);
const char *string;          Your part of the message
```

Example Use

```
perror("Error closing file");
```

See Also

`matherr, errno, stderr`

pow

Purpose

The *pow* function computes the value of *x* raised to the power *y*. The arguments *x* and *y* both must not be zero and when *x* is negative, *y* must be an integer.

Syntax

```
#include <math.h>
double pow(double x, double y);
double x, y;          x raised to the power y will be computed
```

Example Use

```
x = pow(2.0, 3.0); /* x will be 8.0 */
```

Returns

When both *x* and *y* are non-zero positive numbers, *pow* returns the value *x* raised to the power y. If *x* is non-zero and *y* is zero, the return value is 1.

See Also

log, log10, sqrt

#pragma preprocessor directive

Purpose

Use the *#pragma* directive to instruct the compiler in some way. Details are implementation-dependant. Typically pragmas control the kinds of optimization to be performed, whether the intrinsic form of functions should be compiled, and other characteristics of the compiler.

Syntax

```
#pragma <pragma_name (arguments...)>
```

Example Use

```
#pragma loop_opt(on)    /* turns on loop optimization
                           for Microsoft C Compiler
                           5.1 or later */
```

printf

Purpose

Use *printf* to write character strings and values of C variables, formatted in a specified manner, to the standard output file *stdout*, normally the screen. The value of each argument is formatted according to the codes embedded in the string *format_string*. The formatting command for each variable consists of a percent sign ('%') followed by a single letter denoting the type of variable being printed. The complete format specification is of the following form:

```
%[Flags][Width].[Precision][Size][Type]
```

The table below summarizes each component of the format string. The following tables explain the *Flag* and the *Type* fields respectively.

Field	Explanation
Flags (Optional)	One or more of the characters '-', '+', '#' or a blank space to specify justification, appearance of plus/minus signs and of the decimal point in the values printed (see table on page 166).
Width (Optional)	A number to indicate how many characters, at a minimum, must be used to print the value.
Precision (Optional)	Another number specifying how many characters, at most, can be used in printing the value. When printing integer variables, this is the minimum number of digits used.
Size (Optional)	This is a character that modifies the *Type* field which comes next. One of the characters 'h', 'l' or 'L' appears in this field. This field is used to differentiate between short and long integers, and between *float* and *double*. Shown below is a summary of this field:

Prefix	When to Use
h	Use when printing integers using *Type* d, i, o, x or X to indicate that the argument is a short integer. Also, use with *Type* u to indicate that the variable being printed is a short unsigned integer.
l	Use when printing integers or unsigned integers with a *Type* field of d, i, o, u, x, or X to specify that the variable to be printed is a long integer.
L	Use when the floating point variable being printed is a long double and the Type specifier is one of e, E, f, g or G.
Type (Required)	A letter to indicate the type of variable being printed. Table 22 lists the possible characters and their meanings.

Flag	Meaning
–	Left justify output value within the field.
+	If the output value is a numerical one, print a '+' or a '–' according to the sign of the value.
space	Positive numerical values are prefixed with blank spaces. This flag is ignored if the '+' flag also appears.
#	When used in printing variables of type o, x or X (i.e, octal or hexadecimal), non-zero output values are prefixed with 0, 0x or 0X respectively. When the *Type* field in the format specification is e, E, f, g or G, this flag forces the printing of a decimal point. For a g or a G in the *Type* field, all trailing zeros will be printed.
0	For d, i, o, u, x, X, e, f, g, or G *Type* leading zeros will be printed. This flag is ignored if the – flag also appears.

Type	Type in C	Resulting Output Format
c	char	Single character.
d	int	Signed decimal integer as a sequence of digits with or without a sign depending on the Flags used. *printf ("%d", 95);* prints *95*.
e	double or float	Signed value in the scientific format. For example, *–1.234567e+002*.
E	double or float	Signed value in the scientific format, the above example will print *-1.234567E+002* if the *%E* format is used.
f	double or float	Signed value in the format, *(sign)(digits).(digits)*, the example for *Type e* will print *–123.456700* if the *%f* format is used. The number of digits that come before the decimal point depend on the magnitude of the variable, and the number of digits that come after the decimal point depend on the *Precision* field in the format specification. The default precision is 6. Thus a *%f* format alone always produces six digits after the decimal point, but a *%.3f* will print the value *–123.457* which is *–123.4567* rounded off to three decimal places.

(continued)

Type	Type in C	Resulting Output Format
g	double or float	Signed value printed using one of *e* or *f* format. The format that generates the most compact output for the given *Precision* and value is selected. The *e* format is used only when the exponent is less than –4 or when it is greater than the value of the *Precision* field. Printing the value *–123.4567* using a *%g* format will result in *–123.457* because the *g* format rounds off the number.
G	double or float	Signed value printed using the *g* format, but with the letter *G* in place of *e* whenever exponents are printed.
i	int	Signed decimal integer as a sequence of digits with or without a sign depending on the Flags field.
n	Pointer to int	This is not really a printing format. The argument corresponding to this format is a *pointer to an integer*. Before returning, the *printf* function will store in this integer the total number of characters it has printed thus far to output file or to the file's buffer.
o	unsigned	Octal digits without any sign
p	pointer to void	The address is printed in an implementation-defined format.
u	unsigned	Unsigned decimal integer as a sequence of digits
x	unsigned	Hexadecimal digits using lowercase letter, *abcdef*
X	unsigned	Hexadecimal digits using uppercase letters, *ABCDEF*
%	—	Prints *a* %

Syntax

```
#include <stdio.h>
int printf(const char *format_string,...);
const char *format_string;
```

A character string which describes the format to be used

```
...
```

A variable number of arguments depending on the number of items being printed

Example Use

```
printf("The product of %d and %d is %d\n", x, y,
x*y);
```

Returns

The *printf* function returns the number of characters it has printed. In case of error, it returns a negative value.

See Also

```
fprintf, sprintf, vfprintf, vprintf, vsprintf,
stdout
```

ptrdiff_t

Purpose

The *ptrdiff_t* data type is a signed integral type that can hold the result of subtracting one pointer from another. It is defined in STDDEF.H.

See Also

```
* (pointer-to)
```

putc

Purpose

Use the *putc* macro to write a single character *c* to *stream, pitc* is equivalent to *fputc*, except that it is implemented as a macro.

Syntax

```
#include <stdio.h>
int putc(int c, FILE *stream);
int  c;                  Character to be written
FILE *stream;            Pointer to stream to which the  character is written
```

Example Use

```
putc('*', outfile);
```

Returns

The *putc* macro returns the character written. A return value of EOF indicates an error. The *ferror* function should be called to determine if there was an error.

See Also

```
fgetc, fputc, getc, getchar, putchar, EOF, FILE
```

putchar

Purpose

Use the *putchar* macro to write the character *c* to the pre-opened stream *stdout* which is initially connected to your display. *putchar* is equivalent to *putc* with the second argument set to *stdout.*

Syntax

```
#include <stdio.h>
int putchar(int c);
int c;                    Character to be written
```

Example Use

```
putchar('?');
```

Returns

The *putchar* macro returns the character written to *stdout.* In case of any error the return value is equal to the constant EOF.

See Also

```
fgetc, fputc, getc, getchar, putc, EOF, stdout
```

puts

Purpose

Use *puts* to output the null-terminated string *string* to the standard output stream *stdout.* The terminating null character ('\0') is replaced by a newline ('\n') in the output.

Syntax

```
#include <stdio.h>
int puts(const char *string);
const char   *string;     Null-terminated string to be output
```

Example Use

```
puts("Do you really want to quit? ");
```

Returns

If successful, *puts* returns a non-negative value. Otherwise, it returns EOF to indicate error.

See Also

```
fgets, fputs, gets, EOF, stdout
```

qsort

Purpose

Use the *qsort* function to sort an array beginning at the address *base* and comprising *num* elements, each of size *width* bytes. During the sort, *qsort* compares pairs of elements from the array by calling a routine whose address you provide in the argument *compare*. This function should accept two arguments *elem1* and *elem2*, each a pointer to an element in the array. Internally your comparison routine can call upon *strcmp* or other appropriate functions to perform the comparison.

Syntax

```
#include <stdlib.h>
void qsort(const void *base, size_t num, size_t
width, int (*compare)(const void *elem1, const void
*elem2));
const void *base;        Pointer to beginning of array being sorted
size_t     num;          Number of elements in array
size_t     width;        Size of each element in bytes
int  (*compare)(const void *elem1, const void
*elem2);                 Pointer to a function that compares two elements
                         elem1 and elem2 each of type const void *
```

Example Use

```
int compare(const void *, const void *);
qsort((void *) envp, (size_t)count,
(size_t)sizeof(char *), compare);
```

See Also

bsearch, size_t

\r escape sequence for carriage return

Purpose

Use the *\r* escape sequence to move the cursor or print head to the beginning of the current line. To move to the beginning of the *next* line, use *\n* (new line).

Example Use

```
printf("Let's start over\r"); /* cursor goes over L*/
```

See Also

printf, \n

raise

Purpose

Use *raise* to "raise a signal" that creates an exception condition corresponding to the number *signum*. The exception will be handled by invoking a routine that was set up earlier by calling the function *signal*. The *abort* function uses *raise* to create the exception SIGABRT to initiate actions to be taken when aborting a program.

Syntax

```
#include <signal.h>
int raise(int signum);
int signum;                  Signal number to be raised
```

Example Use

```
raise(SIGABRT);
```

Returns

If successful, *raise* returns a zero. Otherwise, it returns a non-zero value.

See Also

```
abort, signal, SIGABRT
```

rand

Purpose

The *rand* function generates a pseudorandom integer with value between 0 and the constant RAND_MAX defined in *stdlib.h*. The "seed" or the starting point of the pseudorandom integers can be set by calling *srand*.

Syntax

```
#include <stdlib.h>
int rand(void);
```

Example Use

```
random_value = rand();
```

Returns

The *rand* function returns the pseudorandom integer it generates.

See Also

```
srand, RAND_MAX
```

RAND_MAX

Purpose

The predefined value *RAND_MAX* is the maximum integral value returned by the *rand* function. It is defined in STDLIB.H.

See Also

`rand`

realloc

Purpose

Use the *realloc* function to alter the size of a previously allocated block of memory to the new size given in the argument *newsize.* The address of the block is specified by the pointer *mem_address.* This pointer must be either NULL or a value returned by an earlier call to *malloc, calloc* or *realloc.* If the argument *mem_address* is a NULL, then *realloc* behaves like *malloc* and allocates a new block of memory of size *newsize.* The memory block of altered size may not be located at the same address any more, but the contents of the block up to the old size is guaranteed to be unchanged.

Syntax

```
#include <stdlib.h>
void *realloc(void *mem_address, size_t newsize);
void *mem_address;        Pointer to the block of memory whose size is to be
                          altered
size_t   newsize;         New size of the block in bytes
```

Example Use

```
new_buffer = realloc(old_buffer, old_size+100);
```

Returns

The *realloc* function returns the address of the block of memory. If *realloc* fails, the pointer will be unchanged and it will return a NULL.

See Also

`calloc, free, malloc, NULL, size_t`

register

Purpose

Use *register* as a storage classifier for integer data types to inform the compiler that the access to that data object should be as fast as possible.

At its discretion, the compiler may use a CPU register to store that variable.

Syntax

```
register <type> <varname>
```

Example Use

```
register int i;
```

See Also

```
auto, extern, static
```

remove

Purpose

Use *remove* to delete a file specified by its name *file_name.*

Syntax

```
#include <stdio.h>
int remove(const char *file_name);
const char *file_name;                    Name of file to be deleted
```

Example Use

```
remove("/usr/tmp/tmp01234"); /* Delete temporary file
*/
```

Returns

If *remove* successfully deletes the specified file, it returns a zero. Otherwise, the return value is non-zero.

See Also

```
rename
```

rename

Purpose

Use *rename* to change the name of a file from *oldname* to *newname.*

Syntax

```
#include <stdio.h>
int rename(const char *oldname, const char *newname);
const char *oldname;                      Current file name
const char *newname;                      New file name
```

Example Use

```
/* Copy "test.exe" from /usr/tmp to /usr/bin and give
   it a new name */

rename("/usr/tmp/test.exe", "/usr/bin/grview.exe");
```

Returns

If *rename* is successful, it returns a zero. In case of an error, it returns a non-zero value.

See Also

`fopen, fclose, remove`

return

Purpose

Use *return* to terminate execution of the current function and return control to the caller. Optionally specify a value to be returned to the caller.

Syntax

```
return;
```

or

```
return <expression>;
```

If the function returns a value, use the statement *return <expression>* to return the value represented by the *<expression>*.

Example Use

```
/* Return the maximum of two integers */
int findmax(int a, int b)
{
    if(a >= b)
        return a;
    else
        return b;
}
```

See Also

`break, continue, goto`

SEEK_CUR

Purpose

The constant *SEEK_CUR* indicates "relative to current position" when positioning the file pointer with *fseek*. It is defined in STDIO.H.

See Also

```
SEEK_END, SEEK_SET
```

SEEK_END

Purpose

The constant *SEEK_END* indicates "relative to end of file" when positioning the file pointer with *fseek*. It is defined in STDIO.H.

See Also

```
SEEK_CUR, SEEK_SET
```

SEEK_SET

Purpose

The constant *SEEK_SET* indicates "relative to start of file" when positioning the file pointer with *fseek*. It is defined in STDIO.H.

See Also

```
SEEK_CUR, SEEK_END
```

setbuf

Purpose

Use the *setbuf* function to assign *buffer*, of size BUFSIZ, instead of the system-allocated one for use by *stream* for buffering. Calling *setbuf* is equivalent to using *setvbuf* with _IOFBF and BUFSIZ as the third and the fourth argument respectively. If *buffer* is NULL, the third argument will be _IONBF.

Syntax

```
#include <stdio.h>
void setbuf(FILE *stream, char *buffer);
```

`FILE *stream;`	*Pointer to stream whose buffer is being set*
`char *buffer;`	*Pointer to buffer (or NULL if no buffering is to be done)*

Example Use

```
setbuf(infile, mybuffer);
```

See Also

```
setvbuf, BUFSIZ, FILE, _IOFBF, _IONBF, NULL
```

setjmp

Purpose

Use the *setjmp* macro to save a stack environment in the *jmp_buf* array named *env* before calling another function. This environment can subsequently be restored by a call to *longjmp*, achieving the effect of a non-local *goto.* When *longjmp* is called at a later time with the saved calling environment, it restores all stack-based local variables in the routine to the values they had when *setjmp* was called and jumps to the return address that *setjmp* had saved. For all intents and purposes, this will feel like a return, one more time, from the last call to *setjmp.* Note that this process does not guarantee the proper restoration of register-based and *volatile* variables.

Syntax

```
#include <setjmp.h>
int setjmp(jmp_buf env);
jmp_buf env;        Array data type where the current calling environment is stored
```

Example Use

```
if (setjmp(env) != 0) printf("Returned from
longjmp\n");
```

Returns

After saving the stack environment *setjmp* returns a zero. When *longjmp* is called with the environment saved by this particular call to *setjmp,* the effect is the same as returning from *setjmp* again, this time with the second argument of *longjmp* as the return value.

See Also

`longjmp, jmp_buf`

setlocale

Purpose

Use *setlocale* to define the locale named in the string *locale_name* for the locale-dependent aspects of your program specified by the argument *category.* The *category* can take one of the values shown in the table on page 150..

Syntax

```
#include <locale.h>
char *setlocale(int category, const char
*locale_name);
int  category;          Indicates the parts of your program's locale-dependent
                        aspects for which you are defining a locale, one of:
                        LC_ALL, LC_COLLATE, LC_CTYPE,
                        LC_MONETARY, LC_NUMERIC, or LC_TIME
char  *locale_name;     The name of locale that will control the specified category
```

Example Use

```
setlocale(LC_ALL, "C");
```

Returns

If *locale_name* is not NULL and *setlocale* is successful, it returns the string associated with the specifed category for the new locale. Otherwise, *setlocale* returns a NULL and the program's locale is not changed.

See Also

```
localeconv, LC_ALL, LC_COLLATE, LC_CTYPE,
LC_MONETARY, LC_NUMERIC, LC_TIME, NULL
```

setvbuf

Purpose

Use the *setvbuf* function to assign *buffer* of a size *buf_size* to *stream*. You can also control the type of buffering to be used or turn off buffering for *stream* by specifying appropriate constants for the argument *buf_mode*. If *buf_mode* is _IOFBF, the I/O operations with the stream will be fully buffered. If it is _IOLBF, buffering will be done one line at a time. Setting *buf_mode* to _IONBF causes I/O to be unbuffered.

Syntax

```
#include <stdio.h>
int setvbuf(FILE *stream, char *buffer, int buf_mode,
size_t buf_size);
FILE *stream;          Pointer to stream whose buffer is being set
char *buffer;          Pointer to buffer (or NULL if no buffering requested)
int buf_mode;          Mode of buffering desired
size_t buf_size;       size of buffer in bytes, if any assigned
```

Example Use

```
setvbuf(infile, buffer, _IOFBF, 2048);
```

Returns

If successful, *setvbuf* returns a 0. In case of bad parameters or other errors, the return value will be non-zero.

See Also

```
setbuf, FILE, _IOFBF, _IOLBF, _IONBF, NULL,
size_t
```

short

Purpose

Use *short* as a size qualifier for *int* and *unsigned int* variables. Note that *short* alone means *signed short int.* A *short* qualifier indicates that the integer data type is at least 2 bytes in size; on some systems it may be longer.

Syntax

```
short <type> <varname>
```

Example Use

```
short offset;
unsigned short array_index;
```

See Also

`char, double, float, int, long, signed, unsigned`

SHRT_MAX

Purpose

The predefined value *SHRT_MAX* is the maximum value of a *short int.* It is defined in LIMITS.H.

See Also

`SHRT_MIN`

SHRT_MIN

Purpose

The predefined value *SHRT_MIN* is the minimum value of a *short int*. It is defined in LIMITS.H.

See Also

`SHRT_MAX`

sig_atomic_t

Purpose

The *sig_atomic_t* data type allows access as a single entity even in the presence of hardware and software interrupts. It is defined in SIGNAL.H.

See Also

`SIGINT`

SIG_DFL

Purpose

The constant *SIG_DFL* indicates default handling of a signal. It is defined in SIGNAL.H.

See Also

`SIG_ERR, SIG_IGN, SIGABRT, SIGFPE, SIGILL, SIGINT, SIGEGV, SIGTERM`

SIG_ERR

Purpose

The constant *SIG_ERR* indicates error return from the signal function. It is defined in SIGNAL.H.

See Also

`SIG_DFL, SIG_IGN, SIGABRT, SIGFPE, SIGILL, SIGINT, SIGEGV, SIGTERM`

SIG_IGN

Purpose

The constant *SIG_IGN* indicates that a signal should be ignored. It is defined in SIGNAL.H.

See Also

`SIG_ERR, SIG_DFL, SIGABRT, SIGFPE, SIGILL, SIGINT, SIGEGV, SIGTERM`

SIGABRT

Purpose

The constant *SIGABRT* indicates that a program aborted. It is defined in SIGNAL.H.

See Also

`SIG_ERR, SIG_DFL, SIGIGN, SIGFPE, SIGILL, SIGINT, SIGEGV, SIGTERM`

SIGEGV

Purpose

The constant *SIGEGV* indicates that an invalid storage address was accessed. It is defined in SIGNAL.H.

See Also

`SIG_ERR, SIG_DFL, SIGIGN, SIGABRT, SIGFPE, SIGILL, SIGINT, SIGTERM`

SIGFPE

Purpose

The constant *SIGFPE* indicates that a division by zero, an overflow, or another floating-point error has ocurred. It is defined in SIGNAL.H.

See Also
SIG_ERR, SIG_DFL, SIGIGN, SIGABRT, SIGILL, SIGINT, SIGEGV, SIGTERM

SIGILL

Purpose
The constant *SIGILL* indicates that an illegal instruction has been encountered. It is defined in SIGNAL.H.

See Also
SIG_ERR, SIG_DFL, SIGIGN, SIGABRT, SIGFPE, SIGINT, SIGEGV, SIGTERM

SIGINT

Purpose
The constant *SIGINT* indicates that the user has attempted to get the attention of (interrupt) the program by pressing a key such as Control-C. It is defined in SIGNAL.H.

See Also
SIG_ERR, SIG_DFL, SIGIGN, SIGABRT, SIGFPE, SIGILL, SIGEGV, SIGTERM

signal

Purpose
Use the *signal* function to set up the routine *func* as the handler for the exception or signal number *signum*. The handler is expected to accept the signal number as an argument. The signal number *signum* must be one of the constants shown in the table. These constants are defined in the include file *signal.h*. If you want to ignore a signal, use SIG_IGN as the second argument to *signal*. Specifying SIG_DFL as the second argument sets up the implementation-defined default handling for the signal.

Signal	Exception condition
SIGABRT	Abnormal termination of program, for example, by calling the abort function.
SIGFPE	Floating point error, such as overflow, division by zero etc.
SIGILL	Illegal instruction in the program.

(continued)

Signal	Exception condition
SIGINT	Generated when user presses a key designed to get the attention of the operating system. For example, pressing Control-C in UNIX or MS-DOS would generate this signal.
SIGSEGV	Illegal memory access.
SIGTERM	Termination request sent to the program.

Syntax

```
#include <signal.h>
void (*signal(int signum, void (*func)(int)))(int);
int signum;                  Signal number for which a handler is being set up
void (*func)(int);           Pointer to handler that can accept an integer
                             argument
```

Example Use

```
if(signal(SIGINT, ctrlc_handler) == SIG_ERR)
    {
      perror("signal failed");
      exit(0);
    }
```

Returns

If successful, *signal* returns the pointer to the previous handler. In case of error, it returns the constant SIG_ERR and sets the global variable *errno* to an implementation-defined error constant.

See Also

`abort, raise, SIG_DFL, SIG_IGN, errno`

signed

Purpose

Use the *signed* qualifier to indicate that data stored in an integral type (*int, char*) is signed. For example, a *signed char* can take values between -127 to +127 whereas an *unsigned char* can hold values from 0 to 255. The *int* and *char* types are *signed* by default.

Example Use

```
int i;  /* signed by default */
signed long int x;  /* signed long integer */
```

See Also

`char, double, float, int, long, short, unsigned`

SIGTERM

Purpose

The constant *SIGTERM* indicates a signal that is sent to a program to terminate it. It is defined in SIGNAL.H.

See Also

`SIG_ERR, SIG_DFL, SIGIGN, SIGABRT, SIGFPE, SIGILL, SIGINT, SIGEGV`

sin

Purpose

Use the *sin* function to compute the sine of *double* argument *x* which represents an angle in radians. You can convert an angle from degrees to radians by dividing it by 57.29578.

Syntax

```
#include <math.h>
double sin(double x);
double x;              Angle in radians whose sine is to be computed
```

Example Use

```
y = sin(x);
```

Returns

The *sin* function returns the sine of *x*. If the value of *x* is large in magnitude, the result may be very imprecise.

See Also

`asin, cos`

sinh

Purpose

Use *sinh* to compute the hyperbolic sine of a *double* variable *x*.

Syntax

```
#include <math.h>
double sinh(double x);
double x;              Variable whose hyperbolic sine is to be computed
```

Example Use

```
a = cosh(b);
```

Returns

Normally, *sinh* returns the hyperbolic sine of *x*. If the result is too large (a *double* variable can be as large as approximately 10^{308}), a range error will occur.

See Also

```
cosh, tanh
```

size_t

Purpose

The *size_t* data type is an unsigned integral type that is returned by the *sizeof* operator. It is defined in STDLIB.H.

See Also

```
sizeof
```

sizeof operator

Purpose

Use the *sizeof* operator to determine the number of bytes that are used to store a particular variable or type of data. When applied to an array (with a reference to element [0]) *sizeof* returns the total size of the array; when applied to a pointer, *sizeof* returns the size of the pointer itself, not the size of the data to which it points.

Example Use

```
image_size = sizeof(image_array[0]);
```

See Also

```
* (pointer reference operator), & (address-of opera-
tor)
```

sprintf

Purpose

Use the sprintf function to format and write the values of C variables to the string given in p_string. See printf for a description of *format_string*.

Syntax

```
#include <stdio.h>
int sprintf(char *p_string, const char
*format_string,...);
```

`char *p_string;` *Pointer to an array of characters where* sprintf *sends its formatted output*

```
const char *format_string;
```
P character string which describes the format to be used

```
...
```
A variable number of arguments depending on the number of items being printed

Example Use

```
sprintf(buffer, "FY 88 Profit = %.2f\n", profit);
```

Returns

The *sprintf* function returns the number of characters it has stored in the buffer, not counting the terminating null character ('\0').

See Also

```
fprintf, printf, vfprintf, vprintf, vsprintf
```

sqrt

Purpose

Use *sqrt* to compute the square root of a non-negative *double* variable *x*.

Syntax

```
#include <math.h>
double sqrt(double x);
double x;
```
Variable whose square root is to be computed

Example Use

```
sqrt_2 = sqrt(2.0); /* sqrt_2 = 1.414 */
```

Returns

The *sqrt* function returns the square root of *x*. However, if *x* is negative, a domain error occurs.

See Also

```
pow
```

srand

Purpose

Use the *srand* function to set the "seed" or the starting point of the random number generation algorithm used by the function *rand*. If *seed* is 1, the random number generator is initialized to its default starting point. This will generate the sequence that is produced when *rand* is called without any prior calls to *srand*. Any other value of *seed* sets a random starting point for the pseudorandom sequence to be generated by *rand*.

Syntax

```
#include <stdlib.h>
void srand(unsigned seed);
unsigned seed;
```
Starting point for random number generator

Example Use

```
srand(new_seed);
```

See Also

rand

sscanf

Purpose

Use *sscanf* to read characters from *buffer* and convert and store them in C variables according to the formats specified in the string *format_string*. See *scanf* for a description of the *format_string* argument.

Syntax

```
#include <stdio.h>
 int sscanf(const char *buffer, const char
*format_string,...);
const char *buffer;
```
Pointer to buffer from which characters will be read and converted to values of variables

```
const char *format_string;
```
A character string which describes the format to be used

```
...
```
Variable number of arguments representing addresses of variables whose values are being read

Example Use

```
sscanf(buffer, "Name: %s Age: %d", name, &age);
```

Returns

The *sscanf* function returns the number of fields that were successfully read, converted and assigned to variables. The count excludes items that were read and ignored. If the string ends before completing the read operation, the return value will be the constant EOF.

See Also

fscanf, scanf, EOF

static

Purpose

Use *static* to localize the declaration of a data item or a function to a program module (file). You can use this to "hide" functions and data from other modules. Static variables have permanent storage; they retain their values throughout the life of the program.

Syntax

```
static <type> <varname>
```

Example Use

In the example below each file has its own copy of the variable *current_index.* Each copy is initialized once, and each retains its last-stored value throughout the execution of the program.

```
/*  FILE1 */
static int current_index = 0;
 main()
{
  :
  current_index = 1;
  :
}
 /*  FILE2 */
static int current_index = 0;
void some_function(void)
{
   if ( current_index == 0 ) ...
   :
   current_index = 2;
   :
}
```

See Also

`auto, extern`

STDC predefined macro

Purpose

Use the *_STDC_* predefined macro to check whether the compiler in use complies with the ANSI standard. This macro should supply a decimal constant 1 to indicate conformance.

Example Use

```
IF (_STDC_)
    printf("ANSI standard compiler.\n");
else
    printf("Not an ANSI standard compiler.\n");
```

See Also _FILE_, _LINE_, _DATE_, _TIME_

stderr

Purpose

The *stderr* predefined pointer points to the standard error stream. It is defined in STDIO.H.

See Also

stdin, stdout

stdin

Purpose

The *stdin* predefined pointer points to the standard input stream—by default, the keyboard. It is defined in STDIO.H.

See Also

stderr, stdout

stdout

Purpose

The *stdout* predefined pointer points to the standard output stream—by default, the screen. It is defined in STDIO.H.

See Also

stderr, stdin

strcmp

Purpose

Use the *strcmp* function to compare the strings *string1* and *string2*.

Syntax

```
#include <string.h>
int strcmp(const char *string1, const char *string2);
const char *string1;          First null-terminated string
const char *string2;          Second null-terminated string
```

Example Use

```
if( strcmp(username, "root") != 0 )
exit(EXIT_FAILURE);
```

Returns

The *strcmp* function returns an integer greater than, equal to, or less than 0 according as *string1* is greater than, equal to, or less than *string2*.

See Also

```
memcmp, strcoll, strncmp, EXIT_FAILURE, EXIT_SUCCESS
```

strcoll

Purpose

Use the strcoll function to compare the strings *string1* and *string2* after interpreting both according to the character collating sequence selected by the LC_COLLATE category of the current locale.

Syntax

```
#include <string.h>
int strcoll(const char *string1, const char
*string2);
const char *string1;          First null-terminated string
const char *string2;          Second null-terminated string
```

Example Use

```
if( strcoll(username, rootname) != 0 )
exit(EXIT_FAILURE);
```

Returns

The *strcoll* function returns an integer greater than, equal to, or less than 0 according as *string1* is greater than, equal to, or less than *string2* when both are interpreted as appropriate to the current locale.

See Also

```
memcmp, strncmp, EXIT_FAILURE,
EXIT_SUCCESS,LC_COLLATE
```

strcpy

Purpose

Use the *strcpy* function to copy the null-terminated string *string2* to the string *string1*. The terminating null character ('\0') of the second string is also copied so that *string1* becomes a copy of *string2*.

Syntax

```
#include <string.h>
char *strcpy(char *string1, const char *string2);
char *string1;           Destination string
const char *string2;     String to be copied to the first one
```

Example Use

```
strcpy(command, "resize");
```

Returns

The *strcpy* function returns a pointer to the copied string which is *string1*.

See Also

```
memcpy, memmove, strncpy
```

strcspn

Purpose

Use the *strcspn* function to compute the length of the maximum initial segment of *string1* that consists entirely of characters not in *string2*. This is the first substring in *string1* that does not "span" the character set *string2*.

Syntax

```
#include <string.h>
size_t strcspn(const char *string1, const char
*string2);
const char *string1;     String to be searched
const char *string2;     String describing set of characters to be located
```

Example Use

```
first_q = strcspn("soliloquy", "q"); /* first_q = 6 */
```

Returns

If successful, the *strcspn* function returns the length of the segment.

See Also

```
strchr, strpbrk, strspn, strrchr, size_t
```

strerror

Purpose

Use the *strerror* function to obtain the system error message corresponding to the error number given in the argument *errnum*. Note that *strerror* only returns the error message, printing the message is up to you.

Syntax

```
#include <string.h>
char *strerror(int errnum);
int errnum;                    Error number
```

Example Use

```
error_message = strerror(errno);
```

Returns

The *strerror* function returns a pointer to the error message. The text of the message is implementation-dependent.

See Also

```
perror, errno
```

strftime

Purpose

Use the *strftime* function to format a broken-down time in the *tm* structure whose address is in *timeptr* into a string whose address is provided in *str*. At most *maxsize* characters will be placed in the string. The formatting is done according to the formatting codes given in the string *format_string*. Like *sprintf*, the formatting codes begin with a '%' and are explained in the table below. The argument *format_string* is expected to be in multibyte characters. Characters that do not begin with a '%' are copied unchanged to *str*. The LC_TIME category of the program's locale affects the behavior of *strftime*.

Format	Replaced by
%a	current locale's abbreviated name for the weekday
%A	current locale's full name for the weekday
%b	current locale's abbreviated name for the month
%B	current locale's full name for the month
%c	date and time representation appropriate for the locale
%d	day of the month as a decimal number (01-31)
%H	hour in a 24-hour clock as a decimal number (00-23)

(continued)

Format	Replaced by
%I	hour in a 12-hour clock as a decimal number (01-12)
%j	day of the year as a decimal number (001-366)
%m	month as a decimal number (01-12)
%M	minute as a decimal number (00-59)
%P	current locale's AM/PM indicator
%S	second as a decimal number (00-60)
%U	week of the year as a decimal number (Sunday is taken as the first day of a week) (00-53)
%w	weekday as a decimal number (Sunday is 0, 0-6)
%W	week of the year as a decimal number (Monday is taken as the first day of a week) (00-53)
%x	date representation for current locale
%X	time representation for current locale
%y	year without the century as a decimal number (00-99)
%Y	year with the century as a decimal number
%z	name of time zone (or nothing if time zone is unknown)
%%	a percent sign (%)

Syntax

```
#include <time.h>
size_t strftime(char *str, size_t maxsize, const char
*format_string, const struct tm *timeptr);
```

`char *str;`	*Pointer to array of characters where result is placed*
`size_t maxsize;`	*Maximum number of characters in* str
`const char *format_string;`	*Formatting codes for converting the time to a string*
`const struct tm *timeptr;`	*Pointer to structure containing broken-down time*

Example Use

```
/* Produce the standard output: Thu Jul 21 19:02:39
   1988 */
strftime(s, 80, "%a %b %c\n", &tptr);
```

Returns

The *strtime* function returns the total number of characters it placed in *str* including the terminating null character. If the number of charters exceed *maxsize*, *strftime* returns 0 and the contents of the array *str* are indeterminate.

See Also

`asctime, ctime, gmtime, localtime, time, LC_TIME, size_t, tm`

strlen

Purpose

Use *strlen* to find the length of *string* in bytes, not counting the terminating null character ('\0').

Syntax

```
#include <string.h>
size_t strlen(const char *string);
const char *string;      Null-terminated string whose length is to be returned
```

Example Use

```
length = strlen(name);
```

Returns

The *strlen* function returns the number of characters in *string* that precede the terminating null character.

See Also

`strcspn, size_t`

strncat

Purpose

Use the *strncat* function to append the first *n* characters of *string2* to *string1*, and terminate the resulting string with a null character ('\0'). The terminating null of the first string is removed and *string1* becomes the concatenation of the old *string1* and the first *n* characters of *string2*.

Syntax

```
#include <string.h>
char *strncat(char *string1, const char *string2,
size_t n);
char *string1;           Destination string
const char *string2;     String whose first n characters are to be
                         appended to the first one
size_t n;                Number of characters of string2 to be appended to string1
```

Example Use

```
char id[16] = "ID = "; strncat(id, name, 10);
/* id is first 10 char of name */
```

Returns

The *strncat* function returns a pointer to the concatenated string, *string1*.

See Also

```
strcat, strcpy, strncpy, size_t
```

strncmp

Purpose

Use the *strncmp* function to compare at most the first *n* characters of the null-terminated strings *string1* and *string2*.

Syntax

```
#include <string.h>
int strncmp(const char *string1, const char *string2,
size_t n);
const char *string1;      First string
const char *string2;      Second string
size_t n;                 Number of characters of above strings to be compared
```

Example Use

```
if(strncmp(command, "quit", 4) == 0) quit_program();
```

Returns

The *strncmp* function returns an integer greater than, equal to, or less than 0 according as the first *n* characters of *string1* are greater than, equal to, or less than *string2*.

See Also

```
memcmp, strcmp, strcoll, size_t
```

strncpy

Purpose

Use the *strncpy* function to copy the first *n* characters of the null-terminated string *string2* to the buffer whose address is given by *string1*. The copy is placed starting at the first character position of *string1*. If *n* is less than the length of *string2*, no terminating null character ('\0') is appended to *string1*. However, if *n* exceeds the length of *string2*, *string1* is padded with null characters so that it is exactly *n* bytes long. You should avoid situations where the *n* bytes following *string1* overlap *string2*, because the behavior of *strcpy* with such arguments is not guaranteed to be correct.

Syntax

```
#include <string.h>
char *strncpy(char *string1, const char *string2,
size_t n);
char *string1;              Destination string
const char *string2;        String whose first n characters are to be copied to
                            the first one
size_t n;                   Number of characters to be copied
```

Example Use

```
strncpy(fname, "tmp12345678", 8);
/* fname = "tmp12345" */
```

Returns

The *strncpy* function returns a pointer to *string1*.

See Also

`memcpy, memmove, strcat, strncat, strcpy, size_t`

strpbrk

Purpose

Use the *strpbrk* function to locate the first occurrence in *string1* of any character in *string2*.

Syntax

```
#include <string.h>
char *strpbrk(const char *string1, const char
*string2);
const char *string1;        String to be searched
const char *string2;        String describing set of characters to be located
```

Example Use

```
first_vowel = strpbrk(word, "aeiou");
```

Returns

If successful, the *strpbrk* function returns a pointer to the first occurrence of any character from *string2* in *string1*. If the search fails, *strpbrk* returns a NULL.

See Also

strchr, strcspn, strrchr, strspn, NULL

strrchr

Purpose

Use the *strrchr* function to locate the last occurrence of the character *c* in the null-terminated string *string*. The terminating null character ('\0') is included in the search and the null character can also be the character to be located.

Syntax

```
#include <string.h>
char *strrchr(const char *string, int c);
const char *string;        String to be searched
int c;                     Character to be located
```

Example Use

```
char line_cost[] = "10 units at $1.20 ea. = $12.00";
total_cost = strrchr(line_cost, '$');
/* Now total_cost will be the string "$12.00" */
```

Returns

If the character *c* is found, *strrchr* returns a pointer to the last occurrence of *c* in *string*. If the search fails, *strrchr* returns a NULL.

See Also

strchr, strcspn, strpbrk, strspn, NULL

strspn

Purpose

Use the *strspn* function to compute the length of the maximum initial segment of *string1* that consists entirely of characters from the string *string2*. This is the first substring in *string1* that "spans" the character set *string2*.

Syntax

```
#include <string.h>
size_t strspn(const char *string1, const char
*string2);
```

```
const char *string1;        String to be searched
const char *string2;        String describing set of characters
```

Example Use

```
char *input = "280ZX";
first_nondigit_at = strspn(input, "1234567890");
/* first_nondigit_at will be  3 */
```

Returns

The *strspn* function returns the length of the segment.

See Also

`strcspn, strpbrk, size_t`

strstr

Purpose

Use *strstr* to locate the first occurrence of string *string2* in *string1*.

Syntax

```
#include <string.h>
char *strstr(const char *string1, const char
*string2);
const char *string1;        String to be searched
const char *string2;        String to be located
```

Example Use

```
char input[]="The account number is ACEG-88-07-11";
acc_no = strstr(input, "ACEG");
/* Now the string acc_no will be "ACEG-88-07-11" */
```

Returns

If successful, the *strstr* function returns a pointer to the first occurrence of *string2* as a substring in *string1*. If the search fails, *strstr* returns a NULL.

See Also

`strchr, strcspn, strpbrk, NULL`

strtod

Purpose

Use the *strtod* function to convert *string* to a double precision value.The string is expected to be of the form:

```
[whitespace][sign][digits.digits][exponent_letter][sign][digits]
```

where "whitespace" refers to (optional) blanks and tab characters, "sign" is a '+' or a '-' and the "digits" are decimal digits. The "exponent_letter" can be any one of 'd', 'D', 'e' or 'E' (no matter which exponent letter is used, the exponent always denotes a power of 10). If there is a decimal point without any preceding digit, there must be at least one digit following it. The *strtod* function will begin the conversion process with the first character of *string* and continue until it finds a character that does not fit the above form. Then it sets *endptr* to point to the leftover string, provided that *endptr* is not equal to NULL.

Syntax

```
double strtod(const char *string, char **endptr);
```

`const char  *string;`	*Pointer to character array from which double precision value will be extracted*
`char **endptr;`	*On return points to character in* string *where conversion stopped*

Example Use

```
dbl_value = strtod(input_string, &endptr);
```

Returns

The *strtod* function returns the double precision value as long as it is not too large. If it is too large, there will be an overflow and the return value will be the constant HUGE_VAL with the same sign as the number represented in *string*. Also, on overflow, the global variable *errno* is set to the constant ERANGE.

See Also

`atof, strtol, strtoul, ERANGE, HUGE_VAL, NULL, errno`

strtok

Purpose

Use the *strtok* function to retrieve a "token" or substring from *string1*. The token is marked by delimiting characters given in the second string argument *string2*. All tokens in a particular string *string1* can be extracted through successive calls to *strtok* as follows. Make the first call to *strtok* with the string to be "tokenized" as the first argument. Provide as second argument a string composed from the delimiting characters. After that, call *strtok* with a NULL as the first argument and the delimiting characters appropriate for that token in the second string. This will tell *strtok* to continue returning tokens from the old *string1*.

Note that the set of delimiters can change in each call to *strtok*. Also, in the process of separating tokens, *strtok* will modify the string *string1*. It will insert null characters in the place of delimiters to convert tokens to strings.

Syntax

```
#include <string.h>
char *strtok(char *string1, const char *string2);
char *string1;              String from which tokens are returned
const char *string2;        String describing set of characters that delimit
                            tokens
```

Example Use

```
next_token = strtok(input, "\t, ");
```

Returns

The first call to *strtok* with the argument *string1* will return a pointer to the first token. Subsequent calls with a NULL as the first argument will return the next token. When there are no more tokens left, *strtok* returns a NULL.

See Also

`strcspn, strpbrk, strspn, NULL`

strtol

Purpose

Use the *strtol* function to convert *string* to a long integer value. The string is expected to be of the form:

```
[whitespace][sign][0][x or X][digits]
```

where "whitespace" refers to (optional) blanks and tab characters, "sign" is a '+' or a '-' and the "digits" are decimal digits. The string is expected to contain a representation of the long integer using the argument *radix* as the base of the number system. However, if *radix* is given as zero, *strtol* will use the first character in *string* to determine the radix of the value. The rules are as follows:

First Character	Next Character	Radix Selected
0	0 thru 7	Radix 8 is used, i.e., octal digits expected
0	x or X	Radix 16, i.e., hexadecimal digits expected
1 thru 9	—	Radix 10, decimal digits only expected

Of course, other radix may be explicitly specified via the argument *radix*, The letters 'a' through 'z' (or 'A' through 'Z') are assigned values 10 through 35. For a specified radix, *strtol* expects only those letters whose assigned values are less than the *radix.*

The *strtol* function will begin the conversion process with the first character of *string* and continue until it finds a character that meets the above requirements. Then, before returning, *strtol* sets *endptr* to point to that character, provided it is not a null pointer.

Syntax

```
long strtol(const char *string, char **endptr, int
radix);
```

`const char *string;`	*Pointer to character array from which the long integer value will be extracted*
`char **endptr;`	*On return points to character in* string *where conversion stopped*
`int radix;`	*Radix in which the value is expressed in the string (radix must be in the range 2 to 36)*

Example Use

```
value = strtol(input, &endptr, radix);
```

Returns

The *strtol* function returns the long integer value except when it will cause an overflow. In case of overflow, *strtol* sets *errno* to ERANGE and returns either LONG_MIN or LONG_MAX depending on whether the value was negative or positive.

See Also

```
atol, strtoul, ERANGE, LONG_MIN, LONG_MAX,errno
```

strtoul

Purpose

Use *strtoul* to convert a character string to an unsigned long integer. The string is expected to be of the same form as in *strtol.* The conversion also proceeeds in the same manner with *endptr* set to point to the character where conversion stopped, provided that *endptr* is not null.

Syntax

```
unsigned long strtoul(const char *string, char
**endptr, int radix);
```

`const char *string;`	*pointer to character array from which the unsigned long value will be extracted*
`char **endptr;`	*on return points to charac ter in* string *where conversion stopped*
`int radix;`	*radix in which the value is expressed in the string (radix must be in the range 2 to 36)*

Example Use

```
value = strtoul(input_string, &stop_at, radix);
```

Includes

`#include <stdlib.h>`	*For function declaration*
`#include <limits.h>`	*For the definition of the constants LONG_MIN, LONG_MAX*
`#include <math.h>`	*For the definition of ERANGE*

Returns

The *strtoul* function returns the unsigned long integer value except when it will cause an overflow. In case of overflow, *strtoul* sets *errno* to ERANGE and returns the value ULONG_MAX.

See Also

`atol, strtol, ERANGE, LONG_MIN, LONG_MAX, ULONG_MAX, errno`

struct

Purpose

Use the *struct* keyword to group related data items of different types together, and to give the group a name by which you can refer to it later.

Syntax

```
/* declare a structure */
struct structure_name
{
        type item_1;
        type item_2;
        :
};
/*declare items of that structure type */
struct structure_name struct_1, struct_2;
```

The first declaration defines a structure with a name *structure_name* and the second one declares two structures *struct_1* and *struct_2*.

structure_name (sometimes called the "structure tag") can be omitted, but in that case all variables of the structure type must be declared within the *struct* declaration:

```
struct
{
      <type> <member_name>
      ...
} var_name ... ;
```

Example Use

```
/* define a structure to be used in a linked list.
   It contains several members including one that is
   a pointer to itself */
struct node
{
    int node_type;
    char node_name[16];
    struct node *next;
};
struct node *p_node, first_node;
```

See Also

union, . (member reference operator), -> (pointer member reference operator)

strxfrm

Purpose

Use the *strxfrm* function to transform *string2* to a new form *string1* so that if *strcmp* is applied to two transformed strings the returned result is the same as that returned when *strcoll* is applied to the original strings. No more than *maxchr* characters will be placed in *string1*. If *maxchr* is 0, *string1* can be a NULL. In this case, the return value will be the length of the transformed version of *string2*.

Syntax

```
#include <string.h>
size_t strxfrm(char *string1, char *string2, size_t
maxchr);
char string1;          String where transformed version of string2 is re turned
```

```
char *string2;        String to be transformed
size_t   maxchr;      Maximum number of characters to be placed in string1
```

Example Use

```
strxfrm(s_xfrm, s_original);
```

Returns

The *strxfrm* function returns the length of the transformed string, not counting the terminating null character. If the return value is *maxchr*, the contents of *string1* may be unusable.

See Also

```
strcmp, strcoll, NULL, size_t
```

switch

Purpose

Use the *switch* statement to perform a multi-way branch depending the value of an expression. In such cases the *switch* structure is more readable than a series of nested *if...else if* statements.

Syntax

```
switch (expression)
  {
       case <value> : statement; ...
       ...
       default: statement; ...
};
```

Use *case* labels inside the statement to indicate what to do for each expected value of the expression. Use *break* to separate the code of one *case* label from another. A *default* label marks code to be executed if none of the case labels match the expression.

Example Use

```
/* Execute different routines depending on the value
   of command. Note the use of break statements to
   keep the execution from falling through one case
   label to another */
switch (command)
{
```

```
    case 'Q': exit(0);
    case 'C': connect();
              break;
    case 'S': sendfile();
              break;
    case 'P': newparams();
              break;
    case '?': showparams();
              break;
    case 'H': printf(helplist);
              break;
    default:  printf("Unknown command!\n");
}
```

See Also

break, case, default

system

Purpose

Use *system* to execute the operating system command contained in *string* from your program. If *string* is NULL, *system* returns a non-zero value only if a command processor (for example, the UNIX shell) is present in the environment.

Syntax

```
#include <stdlib.h>
int system(const char *string);
const char *string;        Command to be executed
```

Example Use

```
system("ls");
```

Returns

If *string* is not NULL, *system* will return an implementation-defined value.

See Also

NULL

\t escape sequence for horizontal tab

Purpose

Use the *\t* escape sequence to move the cursor to the next horizontal tab position on the current line. Tab positions are typically found at positions 1, 9, 17, 25, 32, and so on, but this can vary from one system to another.

Example Use

```
/* Print table headers:
Name                Street              City                Zip
*/
printf("Name\t\tStreet\t\tCity\t\t\tZip");
```

See Also

```
printf, \v
```

tan

Purpose

Use the *tan* function to compute the tangent of an angle *x* whose value is expressed in radians. You can convert an angle from degrees to radians by dividing it by 57.29578.

Syntax

```
#include <math.h>
double tan(double x);
double x;          Angle in radians whose tangent is to be computed
```

Example Use

```
y = tan(x);
```

Returns

The *tan* function returns the tangent of *x*. If the value of *x* is large in magnitude, the result may very imprecise.

See Also

```
atan, atan2, cos, sin
```

tanh

Purpose

Use *tanh* to compute the hyperbolic tangent of a *double* variable *x*.

Syntax

```
#include <math.h>
```

```
double tanh(double x);
double x;                  Variable whose hyperbolic tangent is to be computed
```

Example Use

```
a = tanh(b);
```

Returns

The *tanh* function returns the hyperbolic tangent of *x*.

See Also

```
cosh, sinh
```

time

Purpose

Use the *time* function to get the current date and time (calendar time) encoded as an implementation-dependent value of type *time_t*. If the pointer *timeptr* is not null, the encoded time is copied to the location whose address is in *timeptr*.

Syntax

```
#include <time.h>
time_t time(time_t *timeptr);
time_t *timeptr;           Pointer to variable where  result will be returned
```

Example Use

```
time(&bintime);
```

Returns

The *time* function returns the calendar time encoded in an implementation-dependent manner.

See Also

```
ctime, gmtime, localtime, time_t
```

TIME predefined macro

Purpose

Use the *_TIME_* predefined macro to display the time the source file is being translated by the preprocessor. The time is inserted as a string with the form "HH:MM:SS".

Example Use

```
printf("at ");
printf(_TIME_);
```

See Also

`__DATE__, __FILE__, __LINE__, __STDC__`

time_t

Purpose

The *time_t* data type holds the value returned by the *time* function. It is defined in TIME.H.

See Also

`time, tm`

tm

Purpose

The struct *tm* holds the components of a calendar time. It is defined in TIME.H.

See Also

`time_t, time`

TMP_MAX

Purpose

The predefined value *TMP_MAX* is the minimum number of unique names that can be had from *tmpnam.* It is defined in STDIO.H.

See Also

`FILENAME_MAX`

tmpfile

Purpose

Use *tmpfile* to open a temporary file for binary read/write operations ("wb+" mode). The file will be automatically deleted when your program terminates normally or when you close the file.

Syntax

```
#include <stdio.h>
FILE *tmpfile(void);
```

Example Use

```
p_tfile = tmpfile();
```

Returns

The *tmpfile* function returns a pointer to the stream associated with the temporary file it opens. In case of error, this pointer will be NULL.

See Also

```
fclose, tmpnam, FILE, NULL
```

tmpnam

Purpose

Use the *tmpnam* function to generate a temporary file name in the string *file_name* which must have enough room to hold at least *L_tmpnam* (a constant defined in *stdio.h*) characters. You can generate up to *TMP_MAX* (another constant defined in *stdio.h*) *unique file names with tmpnam.*

Syntax

```
#include <stdio.h>
char *tmpnam(char *file_name);
char *file_name;            Pointer to string where file name will be returned
```

Example Use

```
tmpnam(tfilename);
```

Returns

The *tmpnam* function returns a pointer to the name generated. If the argument to *tmpnam* is NULL, the return pointer will point to an internal static buffer. If the generated name is not unique, it returns a NULL.

See Also

```
tmpfile, L_tmpnam, NULL, TMP_MAX
```

tolower

Purpose

Use the *tolower* function to convert the uppercase letter *c* to lowercase.

Syntax

```
#include <ctype.h>
int tolower(int c);
int c;                   Character to be converted
```

Example Use

```
c = tolower('Q'); /* c will become 'q' */
```

Returns

The *tolower* function returns the lowercase letter corresponding to *c* if there is one. Otherwise, the argument is returned unchanged.

See Also

```
toupper
```

toupper

Purpose

Use the *toupper* function to convert the lowercase letter *c* to uppercase.

Syntax

```
#include <ctype.h>
int toupper(int c);
int c;                    Character to be converted
```

Example Use

```
c = toupper('q'); /* c will become 'Q' */
```

Returns

The *toupper* function returns the uppercase letter corresponding to *c* if there is one. Otherwise, the argument is returned unchanged.

(type) Type cast operator

Purpose

Use the *type cast operator* to make a value have a specified data type. The desired type is placed in parentheses.

Syntax

```
(type) value /* makes value have type */
```

Example Use

```
int i = 1;
(double) i;     /* converts i to a double*/
```

typedef

Purpose

Use *typedef* to give a new name to an existing data type. This can improve the readability of your program as well as making declarations simpler to type.

Syntax

```
typedef existing_type new_name;
```

Example Use

```
typedef int (*P_FUNC)();
/* you can now use P_FUNC as a data type that means
   "pointer to a function returning an integer" */
```

See Also

`enum`

UCHAR_MAX

Purpose

The predefined value *UCHAR_MAX* is the maximum value of an *unsigned char.* It is defined in LIMITS.H.

See Also

`UINT_MAX, USHRT_MAX`

UINT_MAX

Purpose

The predefined value *UINT_MAX* is the maximum value of an *unsigned int.* It is defined in LIMITS.H.

See Also

`UCHAR_MAX, USHRT_MAX`

ULONG_MAX

Purpose

The predefined value *ULONG_MAX* is the maximum value of an *unsigned long int.* It is defined in LIMITS.H.

See Also

`UINT_MAX, USHRT_MAX`

#undef preprocessor directive

Purpose

Use the *#undef* preprocessor to remove a symbol or macro definition currently existing in the program.

Syntax

```
#undef symbol
```

Example Use

```
#undef DEBUG /* removes definition of DEBUG */
```

See Also

```
#define, #ifdef, #ifndef, defined
```

ungetc

Purpose

Use *ungetc* to push the character *c* back onto *stream.* The characters that are pushed back will be returned to subsequent read operations on *stream* in the reverse order of their pushing. You can push any character except the constant EOF.

Since *ungetc* pushes the character into the stream's buffer, any operation that tampers with the buffer or the file's current position (for example, *fseek, fsetpos,* or *rewind*), may discard the pushed-back characters.

Syntax

```
#include <stdio.h>
int ungetc(int c, FILE *stream);
int c;                 Character to be pushed into the file's buffer
FILE *stream;          Pointer to stream onto which the character is pushed back
```

Example Use

```
ungetc(last_char, infile);
```

Returns

If there are no errors, *ungetc* returns the character it pushed back. Otherwise, it returns the constant EOF to indicate an error.

See Also

```
fgetc, fputc, getc, getchar, putc, putchar, EOF FILE
```

union

Purpose

Use *union* to allocate storage for several data items at the same location. This is useful when a program needs to access the same item of data in different ways. The declaration of *union* is identical to that of *struct,* except that in a *union* all data items in the declaration share the same storage location.

Syntax

```
union <union_name>
{
    <type> <member_name>
    ...
};
```

union-name (sometimes called the union's "tag") can be omitted, in which case variables of the union type must be declared in the same statement as the union definition.

```
union
{
      <type> <member_name>
      ...
} var_name ... ;
```

Example Use

```
/* Declare a union that stores a short in the same
   location as an array of two characters. Each
   individual byte of the short stored in the
   union x can be accessed by x.bytes[0] and
   x.bytes[1]*/
union short_u
{
    short sh_val;
    char  bytes[2];
};
union short_u x;
```

See Also

struct

unsigned

Purpose

Use the *unsigned* qualifier with integer data types (*char, int, short int,* and *long int*) to tell the compiler that the variable will be used to store non-negative values only. This effectively doubles the maximum value that can be stored in that variable. Another useful feature is that arithmetic involving *unsigned* integers can never overflow because all operations are performed modulo a number that is one greater than the largest value that can be represented by that unsigned type.

Syntax

```
unsigned <integer type> <varname>
```

Example Use

```
unsigned char data[1000];
unsigned long file_pos;
unsigned i;     /* equivalent to unsigned int i */
```

See Also

```
char, double, float, int, long, short, unsigned
```

USHRT_MAX

Purpose

The predefined value *USHRT_MAX* is the maximum value of an *unsigned short int.* It is defined in LIMITS.H.

See Also

```
UINT_MAX, USHRT_MAX
```

\v escape sequence for vertical tab

Purpose

Use the *\v* escape sequence to move the cursor to the next vertical tab position. This does not work with most video displays and some printers.

Example Use

```
printf("\vf\va\vl\vl\vi\vn\vg");
```

See Also

```
printf, \n, \t
```

va_arg, va_end, va_start

Purpose

Use the *va_start, va_arg* and *va_end* macros to access the arguments of a function when it takes a fixed number of required arguments followed by a variable number of optional arguments. The required arguments are in standard style and accessed by parameter name. The optional arguments are accessed using the macros *va_start, va_arg* and *va_end.* See the tutorial for a step-by-step description.

Syntax

```
#include <stdarg.h>
<type> va_arg(va_list arg_ptr, <type>);
void va_end(va_list arg_ptr);
void va_start(va_list arg_ptr, prev_param);
```

`va_list arg_ptr;`	*Pointer to list of arguments*
`prev_param`	*Name of parameter just preceding first optional argument*
`<type>`	*Type of argument to be retrieved, for example* char*

Example Use

```
va_start(argp, firstint);
first_x = firstint;
next_x = va_arg(argp, int);
```

Returns

The *va_arg* macro returns a pointer to the next argument of given type. The *va_start* macro sets a pointer to the beginning of the list of arguments.

See Also

`vfprintf, vprintf, vsprintf`

va_list

Purpose

The *va_list* data type hold macros needed by the macros *va_start, va_arg,* and *va_end.* These macros are used to allow functions to accept a variable number of parameters. It is defined in STDARG.H.

See Also

`va_arg, va_start, va_end`

vfprintf

Purpose

Use *vfprintf* to write formatted output to *stream,* just as as *fprintf* would, except that *vfprintf* accepts a pointer to the list of variables (in *arg_pointer*) rather than the variables themselves, allowing a variable number of items to be printed. See *printf* for a detailed description of the *format_string* argument.

Syntax

```
#include <stdarg.h>
#include <stdio.h>
int vfprintf(FILE *stream, const char *format_string,
va_list arg_pointer);
FILE *stream;                  Pointer to stream to which the output goes
const char *format_string;     A character string which describes the
                               format to be used
va_list arg_pointer;           Pointer to a list containing a variable number of
                               arguments that are being printed
```

Example Use

```
vfprintf(stderr, p_format, p_arg);
```

Returns

The *vfprintf* function returns the number of characters it has printed, excluding the terminating null character ('\0').

See Also

```
printf, sprintf, vprintf, vsprintf, va_arg, va_end
FILE, stderr
```

void

Purpose

Use the data type *void* in a function declaration to indicate the nonexistence of a return value or the fact that the function uses no arguments. You can also use *void* * to declare a pointer to any type of data object.

Syntax

```
void func (void);
```

The first *void* if present indicates that *func* does not return a value. The second *void* if present indicates that *func* takes no arguments.

Example Use

```
void a_function(void *buffer);
int get_something(void);
extern void *p_buf;
```

See Also

```
char, int, double, float
```

volatile

Purpose

Use *volatile* type qualifier to inform the compiler that the variable which follows may be modified by factors outside the control of your program. For example, the contents of a register in the real-time clock in your system will be such a variable. The *volatile* qualifier warns the compiler that actions performed on *volatile* data must not be "optimized out." You can use the qualifier *const* together with *volatile* to qualify objects that must not be changed by your program, yet that may change due to external factors.

Syntax

```
volatile <type> <varname>
```

Example Use

```
/* The code below shows the declaration of the
   register in a real-time clock.  It says that
   our code can not change the contents
   (*p_rt_clock), but the contents may change by
   itself.  We are, however, free to modify the
   pointer p_rt_clock to point to another long
   int */
const volatile long *p_rt_clock = CLOCK_ADDRESS;
```

See Also

```
const
```

vprintf

Purpose

Use *vprintf* to peform the same functions as printf, that is, write formatted output to *stdout*, when you have only a pointer to the list of variables to be printed (in *arg_pointer*) rather than the variables themselves. This allows a variable number of arguments to be printed. The *format_string* is described under *printf.*

Syntax

```
#include <stdarg.h>
#include <stdio.h>
int vprintf(const char *format_string, va_list
arg_pointer);
const char *format_string;        A character string which describes the
                                  format to be used
```

```
va_list arg_pointer;        Pointer to a list containing a variable number of
                            arguments that are being printed
```

Example Use

```
vprintf(p_format, p_arg);
```

Returns

The *vprintf* function returns the number of characters it has printed, excluding the terminating null character ('\0').

See Also

```
fprintf, printf, sprintf, vfprintf, va_arg, va_end,
stdout
```

vsprintf

Purpose

Use *vsprintf* to perform the same function as *sprintf*, i.e., write formatted output to the string *p_string*, except that *vsprintf* accepts a pointer to a list of variables (in *arg_pointer*) rather than the variables themselves. Thus a variable number of arguments can be formatted. See *printf* for a description of the *format_string* argument.

Syntax

```
#include <stdarg.h>
#include <stdio.h>
int vsprintf(char *p_string, const char *format_string,
                  va_list arg_pointer);
char *p_string;             Pointer to an array of characters where vsprintf
                            sends its formatted output
const char *format_string;      A character string which describes the
                                format to be used
va_list arg_pointer;        Pointer to a list containing a variable number of
                            arguments that are being printed
```

Example Use

```
vsprintf(err_msg, p_format, p_arg);
```

Returns

The *vsprintf* function returns the number of characters it has printed, excluding the terminating null character ('\0').

See Also

```
fprintf, printf, sprintf, vfprintf, vprintf,
va_arg, va_end
```

wchar_t

Purpose

The *wchar_t* data type can hold the entire range of values necessary to represent the largest extended character set supported by the compiler. It is defined in STDLIB.H.

See Also

`char`

wctomb

Purpose

Use the *wctomb* function to convert *wchar*, a character of *wchar_t* type to a multibyte character and store the result in the array *s*. At most MB_CUR_MAX characters will be stored in the array *s*.

Syntax

```
#include <stdlib.h>
int wctomb(char *s, wchar_t wchar);
char *s;                Pointer to start of array where the multibyte equivalent
                        of wchar will be returned
wchar_t  wchar;         Wide character to be converted to multibyte format
```

Example Use

```
wctomb(mb_char, wchar);
```

Returns

If *s* is NULL, *wctomb* will return a 0 or a non-zero depending on whether multibyte encodings have state dependencies or not. If *s* not NULL, *wctomb* returns the number of bytes that comprise the multibyte character corresponding to the wide character *wchar*. If *wchar* does not correspond to a valid multibyte character, it returns -1.

See Also

`mblen, mbtowc, mbstowcs, wcstombs, MB_CUR_MAX, NULL, wchar_t`

wcstombs

Purpose

Use the *wcstombs* function to convert a sequence of codes of *wchar_t* type given in the array *pwcs* into a sequence of multibyte characters and store at most *n* such bytes in the array *mbs*.

Syntax

```
#include <stdlib.h>
size_t wcstombs(char *mbs, const wchar_t *pwcs,
size_t n);
```

`const char *mbs;`	*Pointer to array where multibyte characters will be stored*
`wchar_t *pwcs;`	*Pointer to array of wide characters to be converted to multibyte format*
`size_t n;`	*Maximum number of multibyte characters to be stored in* mbs

Example Use

```
wcstombs(mb_array, wc_array, 10*MB_CUR_MAX);
```

Returns

If successful, the *wcstombs* function returns the number of bytes it stored in *mbs*, not including a terminating null character, if any. If *wcstombs* encountered a wide character code that does not correspond to a valid multibyte character, it returns -1 cast as *size_t*.

See Also

```
mblen, mbtowc, mbstowcs, wctomb, MB_CUR_MAX,
size_t, wchar_t
```

while

Purpose

Use the *while* statement to construct a loop that tests a condition and continues to execute the specified statements as long as the condition is true (not 0). Unlike the case of the *do...while* loop, the condition in the *while* statement is checked first, and then the body of the loop is executed if the condition is true.

Syntax

```
while (<condition>)
{
   statement;
   ...
};
```

A *while* loop with only statement in the body is sometimes written as:

```
while (condition) statement;
```

Example Use

```
/* add up the numbers from 1 through 10 */
sum = 0;
i = 0;
while(i <= 10)
{
    sum += i;
    i++;
}
```

See Also

`do, for, if, switch`

MASTER C COMMAND REFERENCE

This appendix describes the purpose of the commands located at the bottom of the screen in the option bar area. Note that not all of these options appear in the option bar area at the same time; some are context sensitive and are displayed only during certain modes. For example, *Note* and *Example* appear only in the option bar area when a *Note* or *Example* window is available for the screen you are using, *Achievement* is only shown at menu screens and so on.

Achievement

Master C saves a record of your progress in a special file. Select **A** to see this record. A highlighted word or small graphic box character will be displayed next to each section as follows:

a) a percentage between 80 and 100 indicates you have successfully completed the lesson and shows your score.

b) BEGUN indicates you have started but not completed the lesson, or that you have failed the lesson.

c) DONE indicates that you have successfully completed a lesson that did not include any questions, hence no percentage is displayed.

d) REPEAT indicates you have started a lesson that was completed with a score of less than 80%.

e) REVIEWED indicates that you have completed the review sections of a chapter but not all preceeding lessons.

f) A small box character (■) indicates that the section has not been entered yet.

Forward

Forward is used to move to the next screen in the lesson.

Back

Back moves you back a screen to the previous lesson. If you are at the first screen, Back will take you to the point where you entered the current lesson.

Note

Note is displayed when a special *Notes* window is available containing additional relevant information about the current concept. The Note label will flash if it is available.

Example

Example is displayed when a special *Examples* window is available containing related examples for the current screen. The Example label will flash if it is available.

Glossary

Glossary provides on-line access to a collection of terms and concepts related to the C language. When you access the glossary you are requested to type in the name of the word you wish to look up. If the word is not available a list of similar spellings is presented. Once the word is found, a definition is displayed, and you can choose to see a related lesson.

Calc

Calc provides access to Master C's built-in calculator.

Write

The Write command provides the name and phone number of The Waite Group.

Help

The Help command provides access to the help window. From this window you can change the color mapping of the screen to monochrome or back to color; get help on the options that are enabled in the option bar area; and on menus, get additional information on menu items. Your name and serial number are also contained in this window.

Refresh

The Refresh option is used to refresh the screen and remove any windows that are enabled.

Obj

The Objective option is used to enable the Objective window which identifies the main topics covered in the associated lesson and the time required by an average beginner to complete the lesson.

Done

The Done option is used to exit from a lesson or submenu. After confirmation you will be sent to the previous section you were using in Master C, usually an originating menu.

Jump

The Jump option is used to move directly to a particular section in a lesson without having to navigate the menu system. This might be useful, if for example, you are using the book *C: Step by Step*. You can simply press **J**, and follow it with the number of the lesson found in the book, such as 4.4.1. You can also jump directly to a particular screen in a lesson by adding a comma and the screen number, for example to go to screen 12 of lesson 4.4.1, type 4.4.1,12.

Tutor

The Tutor option brings up the on-line tutor which gives you a lesson in using Master C.

Quit

The Quit option exits from Master C after confirming your intentions. Quit remembers where in Master C you have been so the next time you start Master C it will return to that location.

Dear Reader:

Thank you for considering the purchase of *Master C*. Readers have come to know products from **The Waite Group** for the care and quality we put in them. Let me tell you a little about our group and how we make our books.

It started in 1976 when I could not find a computer book that really taught me anything. The books that were available talked down to people, lacked illustrations and examples, were poorly laid out, and were written as if you already understood all the terminology. So I set out to write a good book about microcomputers. This was to be a special book—very graphic, with a friendly and casual style, and filled with examples. The result was an instant best-seller.

Over the years, I developed this approach into a "formula" (nothing really secret here, just a lot of hard work—I am a crazy man about technical accuracy and high-quality illustrations). I began to find writers who wanted to write books in this way. This led to co-authoring and then to multiple-author books and many more titles (over seventy titles currently on the market). As **The Waite Group** author base grew, I trained a group of editors to manage our products. We now have a team devoted to putting together the best possible book package and maintaining the high standard of our existing books.

Master C is an example of a new breed of Waite Group product. This innovative software package does the things that you would want a teacher to do. You can look up C related words in its glossary then ask for a lesson about the word. When you can understand the answer to a question, *Master C* will often present the question in a different format, e.g., a fill-in-the-blank becomes a multiple choice. *Master C* accepts rough or misspelled answers, and you can abbreviate the answer. You can run through *Master C*'s super clear menu system, just as if you were turning the pages of a book. Menus correspond to chapters, and submenus correspond to chapter headings. In fact you can type in a heading number from our book *C: Step-by-Step*, and the corresponding lesson in *Master C* will be entered (plus *Master C* uses less trees than a traditional book).

If you are interested in a specific implementation of C, check our best sellers *Microsoft C Programming for the PC* and *Turbo C Programming for the PC*. For a comprehensive reference to the C libraries, see our *Microsoft C Bible* and *Turbo C Bible*. A list of all our titles can be found in the back of this book. In fact, let us know what you want and we'll try to write about it.

Thanks again for considering the purchase of this title. If you care to tell me anything you like (or don't like) about the book, please write or email to the addresses on this letterhead.

THE WAITE GROUP

Sincerely,

Mitchell Waite

Mitchell Waite
The Waite Group

MCI Mail: The Waite Group ▪ **Compuserve:** 75146,3515

Bix: mwaite ▪ **internet:** mitch@well ▪ **uucp:** hplabs!well!mitch

100 Shoreline Highway Suite A-285 Mill Valley, California 94941 415-331-0575 Fax 415-331-1075

RELATED TITLES FROM THE WAITE GROUP

C: Step-by-Step

Waite and Prata, The Waite Group

The first in the Howard W. Sams Computer Science Series, this entry-level text follows an orderly, methodical fashion to teach the basics of C programming. Designed specifically for a one-or-two semester course in C programming, with exercises and quizzes throughout.

This book moves through the fundamentals of the C language using practical, logical, interactive tutorials, emphasizing today's methods of structured code, step-wise refinement and top-down design. An instructor's guide is also available.

Topics covered include: ▪ Operators, Expressions and Statements, ▪ Character Strings and Formatted Input/Output, ▪ If Statements, Relational and Logical Operators, ▪ Character I/O and Redirection, ▪ Arrays and Pointers, ▪ Storage Classes and Program Development, ▪ The C Preprocessor and the C Library, ▪ The Latest ANSI C Standard.

600 Pages, 7 1/2 × 9 3/4, Softbound **ISBN: 0-672-22651-0, $27.95**

The Waite Group's Microsoft C Bible, 2nd Edition

Nabajyoti Barkakati

The Waite Group's Microsoft C Bible, 2nd Edition provides a thorough description of every function of the Microsoft C library, complete with practical, real-world MS-DOS-based examples for each function. Library routines are broken down into functional categories with an intermediate level tutorial followed by functions and examples.

Included are "quick-start" tutorials, complete ANSI prototypes for each function, extensive program examples, and handy jump tables to help enhance learning.

Topics covered include: ▪ Overview of the C Language, ▪ Microsoft C 6.0 Compiler Features and Options, ▪ Process Control, ▪ Memory Allocation and Management, ▪ Buffer Manipulation, ▪ Data Conversion Routines, ▪ Math Routines, ▪ Character Classification and Manipulation, ▪ Searching and Sorting, ▪ File and Directory Manipulation, ▪ Input and Output Routines, ▪ Drawing and Animation, ▪ Programmer's Workbench and the NMAKE Facility, ▪ New Based Pointers.

800 Pages, 7 3/8 × 9 1/4, Softbound **ISBN: 0-672-22736-3, $29.95**

The Waite Group's Turbo C Bible

Naba Barkakati

Clear and well-written tutorials point out the different purposes and appropriate uses of each Turbo C function to make programming more organized, complete, and powerful. The library routines are organized into functional catagories with explanations that include the purpose, syntax, example call, includes, common uses, returns, comments, cautions and pitfalls, and cross-reference for that function. Unique compatibility check boxes show portability with Microsoft C versions 3.0, 4.0, and 5.0; Microsoft QuickC, and the UNIX System V compilers.

Topics covered include: ▪ Overview of the C Language, ▪ Turbo C 2.0 Compiler Features and Options, ▪ Process Control, ▪ Variable-Length Argument lists, ▪ Memory Allocation and Management, ▪ Buffer Manipulation, ▪ Data Conversion Routines, ▪ Math Routines, ▪ String Comparison and Manipulation, ▪ Time Routines, ▪ System Calls, ▪ Graphics Modes, ▪ Drawing and Animation, ▪ Combining Graphics and Text.

950 Pages, 7 1/2 × 9 3/4, Softbound **ISBN: 0-672-22631-6, $24.95**

The Waite Group's New C Primer Plus

Waite and Prata, The Waite Group

A thorough revision of one of our best selling C titles, this user-friendly guide to C programming is an excellent tutorial for first-time students of C and a good reference for experienced C programmers. It is compatible with UNIX System V, Microsoft C, Quick C, and Turbo C.

The book moves through the fundamentals of the C language using practical, logical, interactive tutorials. It is based on the new ANSI C standard, and all programs include ANSI prototypes. Today's methods of structured codes, step-wise refinement, and top-down design are emphasized. The program listings are available on disk.

Includes: ▪ Fundamentals of Programming, ▪ Compatible with UNIX C and ANSI C, ▪ File I/O and Bit Fiddling, ▪ Sound and Graphics Access, ▪ Arrays and Pointers, ▪ Structured Coding, New Library Functions, and File Operations, ▪ Macro Functions, ▪ String Functions and Data Forms.

638 Pages, 7 3/8 × 9 1/4, Softbound **ISBN: 0-672-22687-1, $26.95**

The Waite Group's Microsoft C Programming for the PC, 2nd Edition

Robert Lafore

This entry-level programming book assumes no previous knowledge of C as it moves quickly through the fundementals of the language using step-by-step hands-on tutorials. The author shows exactly what to do and how to do it, from simple topics to advanced features, moving the reader in an orderly fashion. This new edition is based on the 6.0 compiler and includes a chapter on the newest graphics features, updates to Codeview, ANSI C prototyping, VGA graphics, MCGA control, and details on the QuickC optimizing compiler.

Topics covered include: ▪ Getting Started, ▪ C Building Blocks, ▪ Loops, Decisions, and Functions, ▪ Arrays, Strings, and Pointers, ▪ Keyboard and Cursor, ▪ Structures, Unions, and ROM BIOS, ▪ Memory and the Monochrome Display, ▪ Library Graphics, ▪ Direct CGA, EGA, and VGA Color Graphics, ▪ New Microsoft Graphics Functions, ▪ Files, ▪ Larger Programs and Advanced Variables.

750 Pages, 7 3/8 × 9 1/4, Softbound **ISBN: 0-672-22738-X, $25.95**

The Waite Group's Turbo C Programming for the PC, Revised Edition

Robert Lafore

This entry-level programming book moves quickly through the fundamentals of the latest version Turbo C, using step-by-step, hands-on tutorials to show readers how to write useful and marketable C programs.

Based on the Turbo C 2.0 compiler but compatible with Turbo C 1.0 and 1.5, it contains new information on the Turbo Graphics library, the graphics model, and Debugging Tracer, as it highlights ANSI C features. The language concepts are presented in an orderly, graded fashion to allow readers to move smoothly from simple to the more advanced.

Topics covered include: ▪ Getting Started, ▪ C Building Blocks, ▪ Loops, Decisions, and Functions, ▪ Arrays, Strings, and Pointers, ▪ Keyboard and Cursor, ▪ Structures, Unions, and ROM BIOS, ▪ Memory and the Monochrome Display, ▪ Library Graphics, ▪ Direct CGA and EGA Color Graphics, ▪ Advanced Variables.

700 Pages, 7 1/2 × 9 3/4, Softbound **ISBN: 0-672-22660-X, $22.95**

INDEX

LICENSE & WARRANTY

This is a legal agreement between you, the enduser, and The Waite Group. By opening this sealed disk package, you are agreeing to be bound by the terms of this agreement. If you do not agree with the terms of this agreement, promptly return the unopened disk package and the accompanying items (including the related book and other written material) to the place you obtained them for a refund.

SOFTWARE LICENSE

1. The Waite Group grants you the right to use one copy of the enclosed software program (the program) on a single computer system (whether a single CPU, part of a licensed network, or a terminal connected to a single CPU). Each concurrent user of the program must have exclusive use of the related Waite Group written materials.

2. The program, including the copyright in the program, is owned by The Waite Group and is therefore protected under the copyright laws of the United States and other nations, under international treaties. You may make only one copy of the program exclusively for backup or archival purposes, or you may transfer the program to one hard disk drive, using the original for backup or archival purposes. You may make no other copies of the program, and you may make no copies of all or any part of the related Waite Group written materials.

3. You may not rent or lease the program, but you may transfer ownership of the program and related written materials (including any and all updates and earlier versions) if you keep no copies of either, and if you make sure the transferee agrees to the terms of this license.

4. You may not decompile, reverse engineer, or disassemble the program.

LIMITED WARRANTY

The Waite Group warrants that (a) the program will perform substantially in accordance with the accompanying written material for a period of ninety days from the date of purchase. This limited warranty shall be void if the failure of the program is because of accident, abuse, or misuse of the program. Any implied warranties on the program are limited to ninety days, or, in the case of a program repaired or replaced under this warranty, for the balance of the 90-day period or 30 days, whichever is longer.

AS A PUBLISHER AND WRITER WITH OVER 360,000 BOOKS SOLD EACH YEAR, IT CAME AS A GREAT SHOCK TO DISCOVER THAT OUR RAIN FORESTS, HOME FOR HALF OF ALL LIVING THINGS ON EARTH, ARE BEING DESTROYED AT THE RATE OF 50 ACRES PER MINUTE ❧ AT THIS RATE THE RAIN FORESTS WILL COMPLETELY DISAPPEAR IN JUST 50 YEARS ❧ BOOKS HAVE A LARGE INFLUENCE ON THIS RAMPANT DESTRUCTION ❧ FOR EXAMPLE, SINCE IT TAKES 17 TREES TO PRODUCE ONE TON OF PAPER, A FIRST PRINTING OF 30,000 COPIES OF MASTER C (AT 240 PAGES) CONSUMES 54,000 POUNDS OF PAPER WHICH WILL REQUIRE 459 TREES. TO HELP OFFSET THIS LOSS, WAITE GROUP PRESS WILL PLANT TWO TREES FOR EVERY TREE FELLED FOR PRODUCTION OF THIS BOOK ❧ THE DONATION WILL BE MADE TO RAINFOREST ACTION NETWORK (THE BASIC FOUNDATION, P.O. BOX 47012, ST. PETERSBURG, FL 33743), WHICH CAN PLANT 1,000 TREES FOR $250.

The Waite Group's entire liability and your sole and exclusive remedy for breach of this limited warranty shall be, at the Waite Group's option, either return of the price paid or replacement of the program. You must return a copy of your original sales receipt along with the defective program.

DISCLAIMER OF WARRANTIES AND LIABILITY

The Waite Group makes no other warranty or representation, either express or implied, with respect to the program, the related book, or their quality, performance, merchantability, or fitness for any particular purposes. The Waite Group shall not be liable for any direct, indirect, special, incidental or consequential damages (including loss of profits, business interruption, loss of information, or other money loss) resulting from the use of or inability to use the program, even if The Waite Group has been advised of the possibility of such damages.

Some states do not allow the exclusion or limitation of implied warranties or liability for incidental or consequential damages, so the above exclusions or limitations may not apply to you. This limited warranty gives you specific legal rights; you may have others, which vary from state to state.

Master C uses a NATAL run-time interpreter supplied under license by Softwords. NATAL is a mark of CPDL licensed to Press-Procepic Limited.